D0075725

The Art of Writing for Children

The Art of Writing for Children

Skills and Techniques of the Craft

Connie C. Epstein

Archon Books 1991

First published as an Archon Book,
an imprint of The Shoe String Press, Inc.,
Hamden, Connecticut 06514.

Printed in the United States of America

The paper used in this publication meets the minimum requirements of
American National Standard for Information Sciences—Permanence of
Paper for Printed Library Materials, ANSI Z39.48—1984. ∞

Library of Congress Cataloging-in-Publication Data
Epstein, Connie C.
The art of writing for children : skills
and techniques of the craft
Connie C. Epstein
        p.   cm.
Includes bibliographical references and index.
1. Children's literature—Authorship.
I. Title.
PN147.5.E67   1991   91-32952   808.06'8—dc20
ISBN 0-208-02296-1 (cloth)
ISBN 0-208-02297-X (paper)

To the memory of
Elisabeth B. Hamilton,
a major influence in American
children's book publishing

And
with thanks to
the staff of the children's room of the
Port Washington, New York, Public Library
for their readiness to book talk and
to share their experience "on the front line."

Contents

1

Children's Books Then and Now

What distinguishes a children's book from an adult book? Does the difference lie entirely in the look of the book, or is the writer's point of view different as well? Should the content of children's literature be limited, or should it be as wide ranging, if simpler, as that available to adults? These questions have been asked since the concept of books written expressly for children first emerged, and the answers have changed through the ages as societal ideas about childhood and children themselves have changed. Some believe that children's books should instill socially approved ideals of correct behavior, others that they should offer readers an essentially hopeful attitude toward problems they may meet in the future. Knowing something about the development of children's books and the landmark authors and titles that have shaped the literature will help aspiring juvenile writers today clarify their thoughts about what they want to say to this very special audience.

Children's books in the United States have their roots in the literature produced by the nations of Western Europe. Originally they were not designated specifically as having been written for children, for childhood itself was not considered a separate state of being with its own perceptions, interests, and abilities. Instead, children were thought to be immature, sinful adults, woefully deficient in moral and religious principles, whose literary needs were best met by catechisms that pointed out duties, stressed obedience, and prepared them for a proper death. Bible stories were also a staple of their reading, and books like John Bunyan's *Pilgrim's Progress*, which seems incredibly formidable for early ages today, were thought to be appropriate as well.

But gradually certain titles, because of subject matter or style, became popular with the young, and in time, spurred on by the commercial interest of publishers in creating a new market, a distinct genre of children's books emerged. Among those cited by historians as the first, the one most commonly mentioned seems to be *Aesop's Fables*, printed by the early English printer William Caxton in 1484. The animal characters created to demonstrate the moral points of tales such as "The Hare and the Tortoise" and "The Fox and the Grapes" proved to have great appeal for children, though they were not initially intended for them. In retrospect, this change in readership is not surprising, for adult stories about animals such as Fred Gipson's *Ol' Yeller* and Sterling North's *Rascal* still often end up as juvenile books today along with ones that involve fantasy, humor, and youthful characters.

Taking the date of 1484 as a starting point, the history of children's literature can be said to span approximately 500 years, and it contains many of the most enduring classics. The first picture book is thought to be *Orbis Pictus (World Illustrated)* by John Amos Comenius, appearing in 1657 and offering an illustrated guide to everyday objects like flowers. Others that followed include Charles Perrault's original French *Tales of Mother Goose* in 1697, Daniel Defoe's *Robinson Crusoe* in 1719, Jonathan Swift's *Gulliver's Travels* in 1726, and John Newbery's *A Little Pretty Pocket-Book*, a collection of games, fables, and poems, in 1744. Far from forgotten, the title *Orbis Pictus* now is the name of an award given by the National Council of Teachers of English (NCTE) for outstanding juvenile nonfiction, and the Association for Library Service to Children (ALSC) awards a Newbery Medal to the author of the most distinguished children's book each year.

By the nineteenth century, the United States was publishing its own editions of books for children, and the concept of a separate young audience was emerging. Fantastical themes figured in a number of the early ones, such as *A Visit from St. Nicholas* by Clement C. Moore (1822), a translation of the Brothers Grimm fairy tales (1823), and a translation of Hans Christian Andersen stories (1846). The comic German classic *Struwwelpeter (Slovenly Peter)* by Heinrich Hoffman appeared in translation in 1848, and though its humor is sometimes shocking for modern tastes, it proved to be a forerunner of many behavior books to come. Among the cautionary stories it offered was one about a boy who would not stop sucking his thumb, and so a tailor wielding a pair of shears cut it off. The illustration in full color shows the thumbless boy with blood dripping from his hand to the floor, and underneath is the caption, "That made little Conrad yell."

Until this time, the children's books written in the United States and England were much the same, but then came two stories, published within a few years of each other, whose influence seems to have divided the literature and created two different national specialties. *Alice's Adventures in Wonderland* by Lewis Carroll appeared in England in 1865, and thereafter fantasy increasingly became the province of the English juvenile writer. Classics such as *The Tale of Peter Rabbit* by Beatrix Potter (1902), *The Wind in the Willows* by Kenneth Grahame (1908), and *Winnie-the-Pooh* by A.A. Milne (1926) all belong to this tradition, and the English skill with fantasy continues today. Mary Norton's story *The Borrowers* and its sequels, about an imaginary tiny people who are responsible for the loss of common household items like thimbles, are widely read recent examples. Another is *The Indian in the Cupboard* by Lynne Reid Banks, a tale about an English boy who receives a birthday present of a magic cupboard that brings his plastic Indian toy to life, causing suspenseful complications for them both.

In the United States, however, a trendsetter of quite an opposite nature was published just three years after *Alice* in 1868: *Little Women* by Louisa M. Alcott. After its enormous success, many American writers turned to the realistic contemporary family story for their subject matter, and they have excelled in this form. Some of the classics produced include *The Five Little Peppers* by Margaret Sidney (1880), *Little House in the Big Woods* by Laura Ingalls Wilder (1932), *Caddie Woodlawn* by Carol Ryrie Brink (1935), *"B" Is for Betsy* by Carolyn Haywood (1939), and *The Moffats* by Eleanor Estes (1941). A subdivision of the genre might be called "bad-boy literature," sparked by *The Story of a Bad Boy* by Thomas Bailey Aldrich (1870) and reinforced by *The Adventures of Tom Sawyer* by Mark Twain (1876). Among present-day authors who still find the family a rich source of material are Beverly Cleary *(Henry Huggins, Beezus and Ramona)* and Johanna Hurwitz *(Busybody Nora, Much Ado About Aldo)*.

There have been a number of exceptions to the predisposition of American writers to realism, of course, and perhaps the most innovative was *The Wizard of Oz* by L. Frank Baum, published in 1900. Wildly imaginary, it still was a home-grown product, firmly rooted in the United States through its opening setting of the tornado-ridden Kansas prairie. As Bernice Cullinan points out in her text *Literature and the Child*, Baum combined the English fondness for word play with the American appetite for outdoor adventure to create an original style and form. The plot of a dangerous journey, undertaken with a set group of companions, was a new structure, and it stands alone in the literature of both countries.

In addition to their work in fiction, American authors also developed their own form of nonfiction for children, written to be read as a narrative instead of used as a reference for looking up separate items of information. Once more a landmark book—in this instance, *The Story of Mankind* by Hendrik Willem van Loon, published in 1921—showed the way. It gained a wide readership among the young because of its lively style and received the first Newbery Medal to be awarded by the Children's Services Division (as the section was then called) of the American Library Association. As a result of its success, recreational nonfiction was recognized as a reading interest of children early on in the United States while largely ignored elsewhere in the world. Since then, this tradition of literary achievement in nonfiction has continued, two recent examples being *Lincoln: A Photobiography* by Russell Freedman (winner of the 1988 Newbery Medal) and *Volcano: The Eruption and Healing of Mount St. Helens* by Patricia Lauber (a 1987 Newbery Honor title).

Not only has children's literature produced fine writers, it has provided a home for gifted graphic talent. Throughout the history of the genre, illustrations and design have been considered an integral part of writing for the young in contrast to the largely decorative function they served in the production of adult books. At times, in fact, the pictures accompanying a story have proved to be more memorable than the text, and the art of book illustration has come to be important in its own right, prized by a growing number of collectors.

In England, one of the early artists to establish a reputation through children's books was George Cruikshank, whose illustrations for an edition of the Grimm fairy tales in 1823 first brought him to prominence, and the latter half of the century saw a flowering of the picture book. John Tenniel's drawings for *Alice's Adventures in Wonderland* (1865) are still thought to be definitive, and artists such as Walter Crane, Kate Greenaway, and Randolph Caldecott launched their careers during the same period. Today the name of Caldecott is especially remembered, for it identifies the award given by the Association for Library Service to Children to the illustrator of the year's most distinguished picture book.

After the turn of the century, outstanding artists continued to find satisfaction and recognition in the illustration of children's books. Arthur Rackham (*The Fairy Tales of Grimm*, 1900), Beatrix Potter (*The Tale of Peter Rabbit*, 1902), and Ernest H. Shepard (*When We Were Very Young* by A.A. Milne, 1924) gained renown for their illustrations in England, and fine work was being done in the United States as well. Early admired American illustrators include W.W. Denslow, who created the original *Wizard of Oz* characters, and Arthur Frost, who drew the pictures of Brer Rabbit and his circle for the collection *Nights with Uncle Remus* by Joel Chandler Harris. In Philadelphia, Howard Pyle was writing and illustrating historical adventures like *Men of Iron* (1890), and as his art pupils Jessie Willcox Smith (*A Child's Garden of Verses* by Robert Louis Stevenson, 1905) and N.C. Wyeth (*Robin Hood*, 1917) gained attention, the city became a center for the art of illustration. At nearby Chadds Ford, the Brandywine Museum now has gathered an impressive collection of the original work of this school.

The landmark books created by these authors and artists make up a distinguished body of literature that has proved remarkably enduring, perhaps because the emotional ties of readers to their childhood favorites are so strong. Like practitioners of any art, aspiring writers for children should take time to become familiar with the classic work in their craft so they will be able to build on its traditions knowledgeably. They should not, however, try to imitate what has appealed to children in the past. New voices are needed for new times, and stories that feature bizarre characters talking clever, mysterious nonsense like *Alice* or companions traveling together on a dangerous mission like *The Wizard* risk seeming only pale copies when attempted today. Unless a writer has a genius for humorous word play, the extended dialogue of an *Alice* will pall quickly. Great skill with plotting is needed to prevent the structure of an Oz-like journey from becoming a string of unrelated incidents lacking purpose and tension. A better choice is to create a form suitable for one's own talents instead of trying to follow the models worked out by others.

Writers should also be wary of letting earlier social attitudes toward children influence their work as these ideas are continually changing. Until recently, a common characteristic of juvenile books in all cultures has been their didactic quality, using entertainment to instruct readers in ethical and social behavior. For example, many American children once learned proper table manners and other niceties from a book entitled *Goops and How to Be Them, A Manual of Manners for Polite Infants* by Gelett Burgess, published in 1900. The opening poem read:

> The Goops they lick their fingers,
> And the Goops they lick their knives:
> They spill their broth on the tablecloth—
> Oh, they lead disgusting lives!
> The Goops they talk while eating,
> And loud and fast they chew:
> And that is why I'm glad that I
> Am not a Goop—are you?

Children seemed to find these verses funny rather than irritating, but in the last century this didactic approach has fallen into increasing disfavor with authors, editors, and librarians. One reason may be that the library and publishing professions began to appoint juvenile specialists, and these specialists tended to become advocates of the child's point of view. Less concerned with disciplining the young, they tried instead to understand their problems and appeal to their reading interests. Public libraries created special rooms for children, and librarians were trained to find the best books for them and develop the best ways to serve them. In 1918, the Macmillan Publishing Company established the first separate juvenile editorial department, and other publishers rapidly followed suit. Children's story magazines like *The Youth's Companion* and *St. Nicholas*, edited by *Hans Brinker* author Mary Mapes Dodge for thirty years, were flourishing. Although these magazines have disappeared, they paved the way for such present-day publications as *Ranger Rick's Nature Magazine*, *Highlights for Children*, *Cricket Magazine*, and *Cobblestone*. (For others, see appendix.)

With this development of children's book professionals in librarianship and publishing has come growing admiration for writers able to capture the child's perspective in their work. Gradually the didactic flavor of the literature has diminished and is now considered a weakness that must be avoided if writing for children is to earn stature as a true art. The author Katherine Paterson, two-time winner of the Newbery Medal, expressed this thought cogently when accepting the award for *Jacob Have I Loved* in 1981. She told of an interviewer's asking her what she was trying to do when she wrote for children and of his clear disappointment when she replied that she simply wanted to write as good a story as she possibly could. Her conclusion was, "He seemed to share the view of many intelligent, well-educated, well-meaning people that while adult literature may aim to be art, the object of children's books is to whip the little rascals into shape."

Another highly regarded author who shares the belief that adults should not attempt to instruct the young through their literature is Beverly Cleary. In 1982, on receiving the Garden State Children's Book Award of New Jersey for her story *Ramona and Her Mother*, she made the following observation in her acceptance remarks:

> There are those who feel that a children's book must *teach* a child. I am not one of them. Children prefer to learn what is implicit in story, to discover what they need to know. As a child I was tired of being taught when there was so much room for improvement in adults. If there are any adults in the audience who feel that a book for children *must* have a moral, here it is: Children need to be told in words that their parents love them.

Although the technique of mixing instruction with entertainment is looked down on today, the practice still continues, if with different subject matter, as new issues concerning young people replace those of the past. In the 1970s, the so-called problem novel that dealt with what one critic labeled the "Four D's"—disease, death, drugs, and divorce—was in vogue. At first, these stories were welcomed for daring to dramatize situations that many teenagers were encountering in their lives but that grown-ups were unwilling to discuss with them. In time, however, they became so numerous that readers tired of them and reviewers complained of their evolution into thinly disguised tracts on a single topic: the dangers of taking drugs; how to adjust to bereavement; or whatever. As the popularity of problem novels faded, writers and editors largely abandoned them, but the temptation to guide and protect the young through their reading seems to persist, with the current flood of stories based on ecological themes being the latest example. Yet soul searching about using children's books for obvious didactic purposes is on the rise, and the most-admired writers are those who let their characters speak for themselves and trust their readers to draw their own conclusions.

However trends in socially approved thought have affected writing for children, one classic component that remains the same is that of nurturing. Distinct from the urge to guide, it is perhaps most clearly evident in the much-loved juvenile genre: the bedtime book, whose purpose is to comfort and reassure. Out of the need for a text that sustains interest yet calms at the same time has come the concept book, which explains a simple idea rather than tells a story. Margaret Wise Brown's *Goodnight Moon*, showing that the nighttime changes in a child's familiar surroundings are friendly and natural, is a leading example, and the form is widely used for very young ages today.

What kinds of books do children most enjoy today? Are they the same or different from the beloved classics of the past? Since adults usually select the titles that go into both library and home collections, is there any way to identify which ones children themselves truly prefer? In fact, the likes and dislikes of young readers, though they may not coincide with those of reviewers, have never been a mystery. Their favorites eventually become quite clear, but the process goes through two steps and so takes longer than is needed to establish an adult bestseller. First, librarians and parents buy the books; then they introduce them to their children and wait for the verdict on their choices. The librarian judges how popular a book is by comments about it and by its circulation, while the parent finds out when reading it at bedtime if it will hold the attention of the child. In either case, adults may be trying to lead their charges to certain titles, but in the end they must pay attention to what attracts an audience, for there is no such thing as forced recreational reading or listening.

Aspiring juvenile writers can find out about the reading tastes of the young by talking to their local children's librarian and watching the children themselves as they pick out books and discuss them. If an experienced personal bookseller is nearby, he or she will have much valuable information to pass along on which books, both new and old, are favorites and why. In addition, beginners should learn about the programs developed by professional organizations to promote children's reading and publicize the best work being done in the genre. This knowledge may not be of immediate help in mastering the skills of the craft, but it enables writers to stay abreast of what is happening in their profession and offers a way to reach the interested public when and if they start to publish. A distinguishing characteristic of the children's book field is that the specialists in all the sectors—writers, illustrators, publishers, librarians, retailers—support each other and work closely together.

In recent years, schools and libraries have developed regional or state programs to determine which books children like the best by setting up what are called "child-selected awards." From a list of twenty or so candidates assembled by a professional committee, children are able to vote for their favorite, a winner is announced, and the author is invited to come and accept the honor in person. The first one, known as the Young Reader's Choice Award, was organized by the Pacific Northwest Library Association in 1940. The William Allen White Award of Kansas followed in 1953, the Dorothy Canfield Fisher Award of Vermont in 1957, and since then the idea has spread throughout the country. By now, enough votes have taken place to be able to discern trends among the winners, and, as is true of past classics, themes of humor and animals predominate. The list of writers who have won three or more of these awards in different states and in different years includes Keith Robertson (the Henry Reed books), E.B. White *(Trumpet of the Swan)*, Judy Blume *(Tales of a Fourth Grade Nothing)*, and Beverly Cleary *(Ramona the Pest, The Mouse and the Motorcycle)*. Within the context of the times, young tastes seem to stay remarkably constant.

Today children are able to express their book preferences in a number of other ways too. A national project called Children's Choices that produces a list of 100 child-selected favorite books each year has been developed by the International Reading Association (IRA) and the Children's Book Council (CBC), a professional organization of children's book editors and marketing directors. These lists are printed in *The Reading Teacher*, the IRA's professional magazine, and are available for purchase separately by mail. Classroom book clubs that give children the opportunity to buy books directly, first developed by Scholastic, are expanding as other companies like Dell and Field Publications enter the market. At the same time, the growing availability of paperback editions is putting an increasing number of titles within a child's price range. Responding to this interest, juvenile specialty bookstores that feature programs designed to bring young readers into the shop have become numerous enough to form a professional organization of their own. Established in 1985, the Association of Booksellers for Children (ABC) has grown from 40 members to 800 in five years and become an active force in identifying the books that are most popular with children.

As the social concept of children's rights gains more widespread acceptance, the notion that young readers should be able to choose their own books seems only natural. Now more than ever successful juvenile writers are those who remember that children, not the adults who initially buy for them, are their primary audience.

But do any subject areas remain closed to children's book authors today? The answer is both yes and no, for while writers and editors are ignoring many previously accepted taboos, community book-banning incidents are rising sharply. Although these two trends appear to be contradictory, my feeling is that one may be an inevitable result of the other.

In earlier times, when school and public libraries were almost the only source of good children's books, parents seemed content by and large to leave guidance of their children's reading to librarians and paid little attention to what was being published for them. Recently, however, with the emergence of personal children's specialty bookstores, a growing number of adults have begun to buy books for children and, in the process, become more familiar with them. Most of this new audience is enthusiastic, but some have not liked what they discovered and have initiated campaigns to keep material that upset them out of the library. No longer is the business of publishing juvenile books able to operate in comfortable professional isolation; now it has to become accustomed to the jostling of untrained public opinion. On the one hand, this new visibility of children's literature has meant expanded markets for authors and publishers, but on the other it has exposed them to a far wider range of criticism and to an increasing number of book-banning demands.

Nevertheless, subject matter in juvenile trade books, which can be more independent of pressure groups than textbooks, since they do not have to sell in vast quantities to be profitable, has steadily broadened in the last twenty years to reflect the changes that have taken place in family and community life. For example, when the late Norma Klein's novel *Mom, the Wolf Man and Me* first appeared in 1972, the story was considered controversial because it concerned a household made up of a young girl, her mother, and the mother's live-in boy friend. By now, however, it has been followed by many others that explore unconventional family patterns, and the themes usually are viewed as helpful to children adjusting to new relationships. If objections arise, they may cause problems for local school and library personnel, but their scope is too limited to discourage publication.

Yet is there a mystique that newcomers must learn before

they can hope to write a successful children's book? Must the author use specialized techniques to gain the attention of a young readership? The premise of this book, based on my editorial and teaching experience, is that the elements in good writing for children are the same as those in good writing for adults. At times, however, their application needs to be adjusted for readers with more limited knowledge and experience.

A helpful way to start mastering this craft is to work on five tools of writing, beginning with the smallest stylistic effects and finishing with the creation of an overall structure. First comes *sensory detail;* second, *setting;* third, *dialogue;* fourth, *characterization;* and fifth, *plotting.* To construct a well-paced narrative, the writer needs to make use of all these tools without letting any single one overbalance the others. For most newcomers, however, this kind of control is not achieved instinctively. Some overlook setting in the concern to get a story moving quickly; others allow dialogue to run on too long in order to bring secondary characters into a scene; still others slow the plot down with too much transitional material moving characters from one location to another. By considering each technique in isolation, writers learn to analyze their work and judge what aspects of it need strengthening.

The goal is to become a reliable judge of one's own work, the hallmark of the successful author. At the beginning, the reactions of family, friends, and teachers may provide some much-needed confidence, but these opinions have limited commercial value and, if they should conflict, may even be confusing. Many times, in the editorial office or classroom, I've heard writers respond to a suggestion by saying that another reader offered just the opposite advice. "Who is right?" they ask. "How can everybody be telling me something different? What should I do?" The dilemma is exasperating, and in the end writers must be able to decide for themselves what works, what doesn't work, and why. Although much of the storyteller's gift is clearly intuitive, consciously studying the components of narrative can help one develop that essential ability of self-criticism.

In the following chapters, I discuss the five tools of writing and suggest exercises that you can use to develop skill with them. Designed to focus the attention of students on each technique singly in turn, these exercises should not be considered publishable pieces, but they may help solve problems in a work in progress or lead to a story idea that does in time become a published book. To illustrate points, I cite examples from unpublished work and also from children's books that I either edited or have read recently. Much creative, innovative writing is appearing for children today, and I recommend strongly to aspiring writers that they become familiar with the literature. They will enjoy the work of these accomplished authors and be encouraged to see how the boundaries for children's books are expanding.

The last two chapters survey the range of genres to be found in present-day juvenile fiction and nonfiction, analyze the writing skills that they require, offer advice on how to submit work to publishers, and outline briefly what the writer may expect when working with a publisher on a book. (Addresses of the professional organizations mentioned are given in the appendix.) Although the times are competitive for newcomers, juvenile publishing is a growing business, becoming more decentralized, and it remains open to fresh talent. New imprints without a backlog of material are being started up from scratch, and new small companies are appearing throughout the country, perhaps in reaction to the consolidation of major corporations located in urban centers. For those whose interests, training, and experience draw them to the young, for those who have creative ideas and the skills to communicate them, opportunities still abound.

2

The Five Senses

The *smell* of pine trees carried by a summer breeze. The *sound* of a distant train whistle in the night. The *sight* of a charging, barking dog. The *touch* of freshly laundered sheets at bedtime. The *taste* of a sweet, rich piece of chocolate candy. These sensations evoke memories for most people and arouse feelings that become a permanent part of the personality. The wailing, far-off train whistle may make some feel lonely, perhaps abandoned; the piney fragrance may remind others of a childhood vacation retreat. The moment before the dog shows whether its intentions are friendly or not is tinged with anxiety.

When an author includes such sensory detail in narrative, readers are pulled into the scene as they recall their own associations with the experience; it comes alive for them. They identify with a character whose emotional reaction to the sensation is like their own and say that the fictional person seems real. Yet often aspiring writers neglect to flesh out their story with these details as they grapple with the difficulties of working out a plot. As an editor, I read many manuscripts that were flawed by this weakness and seemed unreal because they omitted the visceral heart of their subject. I can remember one about an African boy sold into slavery and shipped to the Americas on a slave trader. During the entire voyage across the Atlantic, it never took the reader belowdecks to witness the inhuman conditions in the hold: the smells of

vomit and excrement, the sounds of terror-filled cries. Another told of a match in a tennis tournament without describing the temperature of the day or the sweat and fatigue of the
players. Still another concerned a boy working in a dog kennel
but did not mention the reek of disinfectant or the yelping din
at mealtime. Plots may have been structurally sound, characters given appropriate motivation, but the stories remained
uninvolving at best, unbelievable at worst, and had little
chance of publication.

For those who want to write for children, remembering to
include sensory detail in their work is especially important,
because it is the essence of childhood. Impressions are strongest when experienced for the first time, and the child is
constantly being bombarded by new sensations in the course
of growing up: eating new foods, decoding new sounds,
handling new objects. The first smell of a rotten egg or the
first taste of a raw oyster is more vivid than any other, and
these encounters provide a rich, dramatic vein of material for
the writer to draw on. The child character exposed to such
situations becomes more real as he reacts to them, and the
reader identifies with him more readily.

So a helpful starting point for beginners is to work on
their use of sensory detail, equally important in realistic and
imaginative fiction as a primary means to persuade the reader
that the events related could take place. Once this basic
narrative device is mastered, then the writer can move on to
develop skills of larger scale. An exercise that lends itself to
many variations is to describe in 500 words a child's first
encounter with a creature, substance, or object, incorporating
as wide a range of sensations as possible. Perhaps you might
begin with something simple like trying to re-create the airy
sweetness of the taste of cotton candy on paper. Or you might
attempt something more complex like recalling the disorient-
ing effect of watching a speeded-up sunrise on a passenger's
first nighttime flight from the United States to Europe. Picture
a young girl, for instance, bewildered by a dawn transformed
from a calming, majestic light phenomenon into a cinematic

blur, show how the sight distressingly telescopes time for her, and capture her emotional reaction of discomfort and unease.

Another possibility might be telling what happens when a two-year-old deliberately disobeys his mother's instructions and touches a hot stove with his finger when she leaves him alone in the kitchen. If you describe his act of rebellion and the shock of its painful consequences in sufficient detail, you should be able to make the reader wince with your account. Some may question the suitability of including such an incident in a story for young children, whether letting them experience this sensation even indirectly is a cruel thing to do. At times, however, the viewpoint of the writer must diverge from that of the parent or caretaker in order to create the dramatic interest and conflict that a story needs. Beginners often feel that the young should be shielded from *anything* disagreeable or upsetting in their reading as in real life, but they should resist this urge when writing, for it can make their work bland and dull.

In general, the most successful and involving pieces to come out of this exercise are those in which the writer does not name the subject at the beginning, for then readers become participants in the effort of putting clues together to guess who or what is being described. Recognizing that revealing information gradually helps to create suspense, one writer used the technique to rework an introductory passage in her fantasy in progress about a young girl who meets a strange little man dressed in green in her garden. Initially, when the creature first appeared, she described him briefly and identified him for the reader immediately. In the revision, however, she reversed this balance, describing the man more fully but not identifying him until the heroine figures out from the sight and sound of him that he must be a leprechaun. The expansion of the sensory detail drew readers into the story as they tried to solve the puzzle and greatly increased the dramatic effect of the incident.

Or you might choose to picture a smelly, squirmy creature given to an eight-year-old girl to hold and how it leaves a clammy wet spot on her skirt. If it turns out to be a newborn infant instead of an odd household pet, which seems likely at first, you should be able to generate amusement with the surprise. It will also demonstrate that unpleasant sensations causing a strong emotional reaction are often more memorable in story than conventionally pleasant ones. If the girl should find the experience of holding the baby as agreeable as the older family members around her apparently do, the scene would not be nearly as interesting.

Writers with works in progress may discover too that sensory detail is the key to solving a problem scene blocking a full novel. One reported that she had been playing with a story about the ghost of an adolescent boy whose mother had been killed accidentally in colonial times and who now inhabits a remodeled historical landmark house. The daughter of the family who moves into it makes contact with him, and through their interaction the pain of the past tragedy is finally put to rest. But the writer was stuck on her opening until she began to think about the importance of sensory impressions and decided to start with the heroine returning home from school and smelling an apple pie baking in the kitchen. Assuming her mother is the baker, she runs eagerly into the kitchen, but no one is there and nothing is in the oven. She follows the tantalizing aroma into room after room, but never discovers the source until finally it fades away and disappears. The ghostly atmosphere that she wanted to create was established with this one detail alone, and the reader was left wondering what was going to happen next. What more can the writer hope to achieve with an opening?

Often the description of a sensory impression is an effective way to begin a story, bringing the reader into the scene immediately. One of my favorite examples is the opening paragraph of *Tuck Everlasting* by Natalie Babbitt:

> The first week of August hangs at the very top of the summer, the top of the live-long year, like the highest seat of a Ferris wheel when it pauses in its turning. The weeks

that come before are only a climb from balmy spring, and those that follow a drop to the chill of autumn, but the first week of August is motionless, and hot. It is curiously silent, too, with blank white dawns and glaring noons, and sunsets smeared with too much color. Often at night there is lightning, but it quivers all alone. There is no thunder, no relieving rain. These are strange and breathless days, the dog days, when people are led to do things they are sure to be sorry for after.

The discomfort produced by extreme summer heat, the unease caused by too much electricity in the atmosphere, the too-bright light that hurts the eyes, the unnatural absence of sound, all these sensations contribute to a picture of tension before a storm. In only five sentences, the author has created a mood of foreboding that instantly captures the full attention of the audience. What are those mysterious "things" that are going to be happening shortly? The reader plunges into the story to find out.

Another powerful opening that gets its strength from the impact it makes on the senses comes in the novel *Prairie Songs* by Pam Conrad.

> The prairie was like a giant plate, stretching all the way to the sky at the edges. And we were like two tiny peas left over from dinner, Lester and me. We couldn't even see the soddy from out there—just nothing, nothing in a big circle all around us.

The arresting visual metaphor developed here is again completed very briefly, but it establishes a mood of loneliness that transports the reader to this other time, other place. The writer doesn't have to *say* that pioneer life on the prairie was lonely; the reader *feels* it and is anxious to learn whether the two children will be overwhelmed by the vastness surrounding them or not. Certainly comparing them to two tiny peas subtly suggests that they are in danger of being swallowed up at any moment.

Pam Conrad is not only setting down her own impressions

of the unsettled American prairie in this passage, she is imagining how it would affect a young girl and her little brother. No sensory observation is complete, in fact, until the storyteller includes the fictional character's emotional response to it. Often, however, aspiring juvenile writers forget that the reactions of someone small in size are going to be different from their own. Ocean waves loom larger and appear more threatening to a tiny swimmer than to a big one; the childhood home seems diminished to the returning adult compared to the remembered image. Adult-size water fountains are out of a young child's reach as Norman Rockwell showed in his *Saturday Evening Post* cover that pictured a young boy helping his little sister drink from one by getting on his hands and knees and making a human stool for her. These experiences are the flavoring that enables writers (and illustrators) to re-create the child's point of view.

One author who has used incidents based on spatial relationships to good effect in many of her stories is Carolyn Haywood. In *Here Comes the Bus!*, for example, the first grade goes off to the woods one afternoon with bus driver Mr. Riley (Rus) to cut down a Christmas tree for the classroom. All the trees the children pick out are too big to fit in the bus, and finally Mr. Riley says that he will have to make the choice, or they will be there all night.

> The children were silent now as they watched Rus chopping down the tree; their faces were not gay. Such a little Christmas tree, was what they were thinking.
> When the tree fell, the children's voices returned. "It's too little," they grumbled. "It won't reach the ceiling. We want a big one."

But Mr. Riley doesn't listen to their complaints and drags the tree back to the bus.

> Most of the children were inside the bus now, watching for the Christmas tree. When the trunk appeared, they shouted, "Here it comes! Here it comes! Here comes the Christmas tree!" As more and more of the tree filled the

aisle, the children climbed onto the seats. The farther up the aisle the tree came, the happier their faces grew. When at last the rear door was locked, the Christmas tree reached from the front of the bus to the back. The children were all surprised.

"See!" said Mr. Riley. "Didn't I tell you!"

The trial-and-error process of learning to judge size independently of an object's surroundings is something children are well aware of, but adults tend to forget. As a young editor, I missed the point of the situation at first and was expecting something more obvious, more melodramatic to happen, like the tree falling in the wrong direction and injuring someone. Only after rereading the scene did I appreciate its subtlety and recognize how artlessly Carolyn Haywood was able to shed her adult perceptions and look at the physical world from a child's point of view. In her stories, she did not explain the problems of her young characters but showed them with the sensory detail that she embedded in the narrative.

How the narrator creates forceful and affecting sensory impressions in a story involves several techniques. An essential is to pay careful attention to word choice and to be as specific as possible. If a child is tasting a food for the first time, pick out the specific quality that characterizes it. Is it salty, sour, sweet, or bitter? Does it burn like the tang of a sharp mustard? Is the flavor unexpected as when someone eats an innocent garnish of sweet pepper, and it turns out to be the Mexican variety instead? Taking the short cut of summing up the general effect vaguely as *delicious* or *unpleasant* will not tell readers very much, and the strength of their identification with the situation will be undermined.

Being forced to eat something one dislikes is a universal problem of childhood, and a writer who has not forgotten the experience is Beverly Cleary. In her book *Ramona Quimby, Age 8*, she describes a Sunday night dinner during which Ramona and her older sister, Beezus, almost make the strategic error of eating a meat that they have declared taboo. What bothers them, a few well-chosen details reveal, is the way the meat looks rather than the way it tastes, and they feel tricked when their mother takes advantage of their prejudice.

> Ramona succeeded in cutting a bite of meat the way her parents thought proper. It was unusually tender and not the least bit stringy like some pot roasts her mother had prepared. It tasted good, too. "Yummy," said Ramona.
>
> The family ate in contented silence until Beezus pushed aside her gravy with the side of her fork. Gravy was fattening, and although Beezus was slender, even skinny, she was taking no chances.
>
> "Mother!" Beezus's voice was accusing. "This meat has a rough surface!"
>
> "It does?" answered Mrs. Quimby innocently.
>
> Ramona understood her mother was trying to hide something when she saw her parents exchange their secret-sharing glance. She too scraped aside her gravy. Beezus was right. One edge of her meat was covered with tiny bumps.
>
> "This meat is tongue." Beezus pushed her serving aside with her fork. "I don't like tongue."
>
> "Tongue!" Like Beezus, Ramona pushed her meat aside. "Yuck," she said.
>
> "Girls, stop being silly." Mrs. Quimby's voice was sharp.

This particular contest of wills is a draw, for Beezus and Ramona don't eat their tongue, but they get no substitute either. Only the cat Picky-picky ("I wonder," says Mrs. Quimby, "why we named the *cat* Picky-picky.") is the clear winner as there are more leftovers than usual for him to eat.

Other sensory experiences should be observed just as specifically. If a character sleeping in a strange house is awakened in the middle of the night by a fire alarm going off in the firehouse down the street, he may be frightened by it. To make the reader feel the shock, the writer needs to report the sound in more detail than simply as a loud noise. It will have a quality (harsh and blaring), intensity (ear-shattering), and pitch (undulating); a description that combines all three elements will create a more dramatic effect. Smells are equally complex and come in a number of varieties including flowery, fruity, spicy, putrid, resinous, and acrid. The appearance of an object depends on factors such as the amount of daylight falling on it, its color, and whether it emits light (sparkles) or reflects it (the sheen). Textures may be hard or soft, rough or smooth, hot or cold, wet or dry.

Fantasy, in particular, needs specific detail to persuade the reader to suspend disbelief, and not surprisingly some of the most vivid descriptive writing is found in this genre. Robert C. O'Brien's story *Mrs. Frisby and the Rats of NIMH*, for example, is admired for its visual clarity as in this portrayal of the fearsome cat Dragon, who terrorizes the wild animals of the woods:

> He was enormous, with a huge, broad head and a large mouth full of curving fangs, needle sharp. He had seven claws on each foot and a thick, furry tail, which lashed angrily from side to side. In color he was orange and white, with glaring yellow eyes; and when he leaped to kill, he gave a high, strangled scream that froze his victims where they stood.

The specific details of size, color, and sound make Dragon seem very real indeed and add to the credibility of this tale that earned its author the Newbery Medal in 1972.

But making a sensory impression specific does not mean including everything about it in the narrative. The writer is incorporating this detail into a scene in order to create a mood, so another essential is to select only those characteristics that will contribute to the effect that is wanted. If all aspects, both pleasant and unpleasant, are described, they will cancel each other out, and the special atmosphere needed to reinforce the plot will be lost. In her novel *A Chance Wild Apple*, Marian Potter tells how a farm family in the Ozark Mountains of the 1930s celebrates Christmas. The McCrackens go to a neighboring farm for the day in a wagon pulled by their horse, Patsy. After a good meal and the reading aloud of *A Christmas*

Carol, the holiday comes to a close, and they return home just
as the sun sets. Here is how the author pictures what Maureen
and her younger brother, Walter, see:

> McCrackens left early enough for Patsy to have plenty
> of time to get them home for chores before dark. The wind
> had died down, and the sun broke through the clouds to
> glow like a woods fire through the black tree trunks in the
> west. Maureen and Walter watched it until it burned away,
> leaving a sky gray as ash.
> "Christmas is over," Walter said.

A beautiful sunset goes through many shades and takes
many shapes from onset to afterglow, but out of all this
myriad detail the author has chosen to concentrate on what
the sky looks like when the color is gone. She has selected this
particular image because it creates a wistful sense of loss, and
with it she makes the reader understand how the children feel
when the much-anticipated holiday is over. Conveying an
emotion in this way is a more direct and powerful technique
than relating the feelings of a character after the moment has
passed.

Another reason why this description of the sunset holds
more interest than many is that the author has used the simile
of a fire to reinforce her image. She does not have to tell the
reader what colors Maureen and Walter see in the sky, or
what shape they take; the "woods fire" draws an immediate
picture and leads to the metaphor of the ashy remains that
both a sunset and fire leave behind. Writers should be alert to
whatever comparisons come to mind when re-creating their
observations in a story, and the more unusual they are the
better. Connections are more memorable because of their
originality. Clichés are boring and should be avoided.

The Newbery-winning writer Paula Fox uses such connections to good advantage in her novel *Lily and the Lost Boy*, set
on the Greek island of Thasos. At one point, she pictures
what the young American heroine sees from the balcony of
her rented house on a silvery moonlit night.

> Amber lights, glowing along the wharf and in front of
> tavernas, pulsed like little heartbeats, the heartbeats of
> rabbits throbbing away inside the dark.

Eleven-year-old Lily loves the island more than any place she
has ever been, and yet some things about it frighten her. How
effectively the author captures the ambiguity of her feelings
by connecting the beauty of the sparkling lights with the
timidity of the vulnerable animal hiding in the dark. The
unusual simile is arresting and gives the scene a haunting
quality that marks the atmosphere of the story.

The storyteller is a role player, always imagining how an
experience is going to affect the senses and emotions of
someone else, and how he or she will respond. To stretch
one's imagination, a helpful exercise is to describe how a
person deprived of one of the senses might react to a situation;
how someone blind, for example, might feel crossing a busy
city street. Writers must be able to take this leap in point of
view for a wide range of characters, with very different
personalities and very different backgrounds.

A leap in point of view that has always impressed me is
the one accomplished in the novel *Pulga*, a winner of the
Batchelder Award given for the best translated children's book
of the year, written by Siny R. van Iterson. The protagonist
is a puny-sized urchin (*pulga* means *flea* in Spanish) roaming
the streets of Bogotá, Colombia, and the author a middle-aged
Dutch woman, born in the Caribbean but schooled in Hol-
land. Somehow she was able to transcend differences of age,
gender, culture, and education to write a convincing story
about the boy's struggles to survive. The plot concerns Pulga's
opportunity to escape the prison of slum life when a chance
encounter gives him a job as a truck driver's assistant. Here is
the scene in which van Iterson dramatizes his feelings of
release.

> On a sudden impulse, he took off his stinking rags and
> flung them on the ground along the edge of the brook.
> Stark-naked he walked to the waterfall and stood under it.

He let the water splash down on him, over his shoulders and his back. He stretched out his arms. Then he bent down, scooped up a handful of fine sand from under the pebbles and began to scour his body. The water streamed down over him. His skin prickled, and his blood began to tingle. He was alive, and his name was Francisco José!

In those few moments of sensory experience, the reader shares Pulga's emotions more directly than if the narrator had expressed them in conscious thought or dialogue. One feels that a rebirth is occurring, although the character is hardly aware yet of what is happening.

Rarely does the style and craftsmanship of a writer appear fully developed. Most must work to refine their technique, and the first step for the beginner is to remember to make full use of the five senses: sight, sound, smell, taste, and touch. They form the foundation that supports the three major narrative elements of setting, characterization, and plotting and enable the storyteller to breathe life into the tale.

3

The Setting

A romance that takes place in a Grecian countryside suffused with the scent of lemon trees. A tale of survival in which the hero must find his way out of a trackless, frigid north Canadian forest. A family story that portrays the rigors of eking out a living from a red-dirt farm in Georgia. A historical novel about the adventures of a black cowboy working in the nineteenth-century Texas badlands. In all these books, the setting is a prime ingredient, affecting the action of the plot and the personality of the characters. In every piece of fiction, in fact, setting is one of the three major elements—along with characterization and plot—that the writer must weave together to create the narrative.

Even the most exotic setting, however, needs to be described in specific detail if it is to come through as a strong presence in a story. What makes these examples arresting is that they are specific, not that they involve places most people will never have a chance to see for themselves. Those writers who visualize their scenes and remember to picture them for the reader are able to make the most commonplace settings memorable because they re-create the look, sound, and smell of them freshly, as if they were observing them for the first time. Nothing could be more ordinary, for instance, than the New York City subway system that is the setting for Felice Holman's novel *Slake's Limbo* about a homeless urban boy, yet the sharply realized background of this underground world is a large part of the reason why the story is so effective.

Still, when a story is set in a familiar locale, beginning writers often neglect to describe the surroundings for the reader. Either they take them for granted—surely everyone knows what the inside of a school looks like—or they seem too minor to mention. But all settings, no matter how unremarkable, can be made individual, and skillful visualization is not only essential for authenticity, it fixes what is happening in the reader's memory. Most children attend school, but classrooms can be bright or dreary, crowded or spacious, new or dingy. Writers should always have a picture of their scene in mind and remember to show it as they tell what people are doing and saying. As an editor, the most frequent omission I noticed in manuscripts submitted to me was a well-developed background for the narrative, especially when the author had lived where the story was set for many years and apparently had stopped observing his or her environment long ago. Usually the lack of imagery made the work colorless and ruled it out as a possibility for publication.

So writers should keep in mind the importance of choosing a specific setting for a story and consider carefully how to visualize it for the reader. The major descriptive details are likely to concern the sights, sounds, and smells of the scene taking place, for they are the ones that the observer often notices first. Then, if the writer moves in to look at the characters and action more closely, the minor details of taste and touch may also become involved. In effect, the overall background for a narrative is created by enlarging on the smaller sensory impressions that you have already worked on. To help yourself take this next step, try the exercise of describing in 500 words how a child feels when encountering a new setting that evokes a strong emotion: fear, joy, excitement, anger, pity, to name a few.

Perhaps because I live on Long Island, New York, where children are apt to be introduced to the seashore at a young age, I often suggest the ocean as a frequent subject for this exercise. Beware the pitfall, however, of picturing the least important parts of the scene first and the most important last. Sometimes writers describe the grains of sand the child steps on initially, then the bathers and their paraphernalia occupying the beach, and finally the water and waves. This sequence may be in order of contact, but it is the reverse of the impact that the ocean makes on most newcomers. Instead, one usually registers the sight and sound of the surf first, then the extent of the beach, and lastly the texture of the gritty substance underfoot. Just as plot needs to be structured so does description, and a good guideline to follow for creating the greatest dramatic effect is to start with the largest impressions and descend in order to the smallest, the way most people respond to a new scene.

Out of the many exercises I have read, the most successful have been ones that offered an emotional surprise; that is, the characters in the sketch are affected by the setting in an unpredictable way. To compose a scene in which the observer is moved by the beauty of a fiery sunrise is pleasant but not especially memorable; the reader expects this reaction. If the character feels apprehension instead, because it portends bad weather to come, the reader will probably pay more attention because the linkage is less familiar.

One student demonstrated this principle when she chose the introduction of a child to Disneyland as the subject of her exercise. Father, mother, and two-year-old approach the entrance to the park and are welcomed by a large, noisy cast of costumed characters, including witches, goblins, Mickey, and his many friends. Excited by the promise of wondrous sights to see, the parents take for granted that the child will find the commotion inviting too. But the little girl is terrified, starts to cry, and turns away from the scene ahead. Stubbornly she refuses to have anything more to do with Disneyland at all, and the long-planned-for trip comes to a sudden, unanticipated end. I was amused by the depiction of the crestfallen parents—everyone can identify with the common mistake of overestimating a child's readiness for a new experience—and

found the surprise of having a treat turn out to be a disappointment more interesting than an account of a happy, untroubled
outing.

Sometimes readers will remember a story more for the
feelings that its setting arouses than for the details of what the
characters say and do. One manuscript I can still recall reading
as an editor was the translation of a Russian story set in
Siberia, submitted by a translator as a prospect for publication
in the United States. It involved a little girl who has to spend
a winter in lonely isolation in the frozen tundra land for
reasons that escape me now. What stays in my mind, however,
is the scene in which she ventures from her hut one day and
discovers that suddenly spring has arrived. Overnight, wild
flowers have appeared everywhere she looks, as if by magic,
and she runs through them almost crazed by sensations of joy
and release. The rest of the plot seemed too weak to have the
chance of attracting an American audience, so I declined it,
but that one passage had the ring of absolute authenticity that
is what every writer strives to create in a story.

To achieve this authenticity, writers must know a setting
through experience or find out about it by means of first-hand
research. So familiarity with an unusual or colorful place is
an asset for beginners to consider when they are deciding
what kind of story they want to write. I remember receiving
a letter from a woman whose husband worked for the Forestry
Service and was stationed in Alaska for a number of years.
While there, she gathered a wealth of information about
wolves, and she described briefly some of her experiences in
the wild with them. Now she had incorporated this background into a story about an orphaned Native American boy
raised by a wolf family and was looking for an interested
publisher. I asked to see it, almost entirely because of the
credentials she was able to offer, and was glad that I did. The
author, Jean Thompson, had created a completely believable
tale out of material that at times bordered on the fantastic,
and in due course the company brought it out successfully
under the title of *Brother of the Wolves*.

Writers should not feel limited, however, to locales that they are already familiar with. As young adult novelist Richard Peck likes to advise, don't write only about what you know, but what you can find out about. If a plot requires a scene in a city the author has not visited, then he can go there and look up the streets, buildings, and neighborhoods needed to visualize the action to come. For her Civil War story *Shades of Gray*, Carolyn Reeder says that she explored the Virginia Piedmont until she could picture the view from every window of the house that becomes her protagonist's home. The important thing to remember is never to fake a setting, for lack of detail usually becomes quickly apparent and destroys the credibility of the story.

When selecting a setting for a story, writers have several types to choose from, and for students I group them in three categories. The first and most obvious is the landscape, or outdoor environment, which can be natural, as a mountain range, or man-made, as a large city. Details in its portrayal will continually change according to conditions of climate, weather, and amount of daylight, so it does not have to remain static as the plot progresses, and beginners should remember that the more variations presented the more interesting their backdrop will be. They should envision a specific time of year and time of day for each scene, establishing with these elements an atmosphere that will enhance the dramatic action.

In the picture book *Porcupine Stew*, the author Beverly Major wanted to create an ethereal mood that will set the stage for a fantasy, so she opened the story during the twilight hours of a summer night. It begins with a little boy named Thomas finding a porcupine on a "silver-soft summer evening" and showing it to Grandpa. The action then continues:

> "Time for bed, Thomas," said Grandpa, and they walked home through the magic twilight while fireflies glimmered, lighting their way while white moths flickered, and the whispery little breeze crooned through the summer-dried grass.

Later in the night Thomas is enticed from his bedroom by a dancing shadow and pays a visit to the Porcupine Parade and Picnic with his cat, True Blue. Here is how the author describes the same countryside as seen in the dark in order to deepen the feeling of mystery.

> Outside the grass was wet with dew. In the field, the rows of hay glistened like caramel spun sugar under the moon. Thomas followed True to the edge of the birch thicket.
>
> In the mossy hollow beneath the birches stood a ticket booth, decorated with lovely blue scallops and curlicues and turnings. Under the ticket window was a sign:
>
> Follow The Dream
> Admission: a Lot

The most familiar landscapes sometimes seem magical during a summer night, and Major uses this perception to persuade the reader to accept her imaginary dream world. She meshes setting, time of year, and time of day to make the fantasy work.

But action can take place indoors as well as outdoors, and the second group of settings to consider concerns interior surroundings. This type of background can be particularly important in a family story, a staple of children's literature, because the kind of home the family lives in has much to do with the emotional interaction among the characters. So writers should take time in advance to envision a specific home for their family and then make sure to include details that will enable the reader to visualize it too. A small apartment housing a large family will create a crowded, harried atmosphere while a country mansion can produce the opposite effect of loneliness and isolation.

An example of a powerful interior setting that focuses and intensifies the dramatic action can be found in the novel *After the First Death* by Robert Cormier. The plot involves the hijacking of a school bus by political terrorists as a teenage girl is driving a group of five- and six-year-olds to summer camp. For most of the story, the characters are confined to the inside of the bus, and the claustrophobic atmosphere that builds up establishes a mood of mounting dread and tension. After the capture in the morning, the windows of the bus are taped, the children are fed drugged candy, and the driver, Kate, is ordered to keep them under control. By afternoon, rescue forces are in place, negotiations have begun, but in the meantime there is nothing to do but wait.

> The children were still subdued, dozing in the dimness of the bus. The day had turned cloudy. The absence of sun and the blocking out of light by the tape gave the interior of the bus an aspect of twilight. This fake dusk softened the sharp edges of things, and Kate found herself growing drowsy on occasion. The afternoon was at a standstill, the bus surrounded by silence except for the occasional howl of a siren or throb of a hovering helicopter.

The emotional effect created by the gloomy quiet is one of lassitude and frustration, an uncomfortable pause between the initial moments of horror and fearful recognition that worse may lie ahead. Each change of mood from scene to scene is heightened by the suffocating surroundings that grow hotter and smellier as the tale progresses.

The third group of settings is far less tangible in nature; it draws on the cultural background of characters. In fiction about people of other lands, observations on their customs— how they eat, celebrate holidays, dress, behave toward family members—add richness and authenticity to the narrative. People with different cultural orientation are common in the United States too, and bringing them together in a story can produce interesting dramatic tension. I remember, for example, a scene that contrasted Italian and American mealtime customs in a teenage novel I edited called *Almost Like Sisters* by Betty Cavanna. The heroine goes to the family of her Italian boyfriend for Thanksgiving dinner, but is totally unprepared for the exuberance of the conversation, the confusion of passing plates, the jumping up and down from the table to refill serving dishes. It is like no other meal she has ever had, yet while slightly shattered, she still enjoys the tumult thoroughly. After a number of years, this passage from the story is the one that stays in my mind most clearly.

Another example is Laurence Yep's memorable story *Dragonwings* about a young boy who comes to the Land of the Golden Mountain where white demons live (California) from the Middle Kingdom (China) in 1903. The plot concerns the bitter clash between the cultures, and incidents run the gamut from the amusing (Moon Shadow is horrified when asked to drink cow's milk, which he considers urine) to the tragic (demon boys are constantly on the prowl for a chance to stone a lone young Chinese). A likeable boy with spunk and humor, Moon Shadow is a character American readers can identify with, despite his unfamiliar beliefs, and through his eyes they gain a broader perspective on their own customs and ways of behaving.

A question about setting that writers sometimes struggle with is whether to make it real or imaginary. If asked for editorial advice, I usually opt for the factual as I feel that locating action in an actual place helps the author make the story convincing. Sometimes a single name—too unusual to have been invented—is sufficient as in the case of the books about Henry, Beezus, and Ramona by Beverly Cleary. They are set in Portland, Oregon, where the author grew up, but the only clue is the name Klickitat Street, which a visitor can still find today.

But naming a real place can pose difficulties for the author if he or she is planning to draw a highly critical portrait of it. I recall an instance when one of the young adult writers on the Morrow list was beginning a novel based on her son's experiences during a year of teaching at an inner-city school in the Northeast. Since the setting was such an important part of the story, I suggested that she identify it, but she was reluctant to single out the school system for what she felt were general problems, and I could certainly understand the reasons for her decision. The choice is a personal one for the writer—there is no right or wrong—but it is something to consider carefully.

When discussing the need to incorporate setting into fiction, beginners sometimes express their concern that children are bored by description and will skip over those parts that are not action or dialogue. My answer is that then the writer has not integrated the background into the narrative fully; when done skillfully, it cannot be separated from what characters are saying and doing and certainly cannot be skipped over.

A recent example is the novel *Charley Skedaddle* by Patricia Beatty, 1987 winner of the Scott O'Dell Award for historical fiction. It follows the fortunes of an under-aged Union drummer boy from New York City in the Civil War, and the first half revolves around some of the famous campaigns fought in Virginia's Shenandoah Valley. But the second half moves to the Blue Ridge Mountains, where Charley hides out after deserting under fire, and this far less written-about locale is what makes the book stand out from other Civil War stories. Beatty describes Charley's first impressions of the countryside as follows:

> As he climbed in the late afternoon, Charley felt the mountains around him. They weren't like the Wilderness, filled with evil smells and memories, but all the same, they were frightening. Their enormous forested bulk, towering over the road on both sides of him as well as ahead and behind, made him feel hemmed in. He sensed that the trees watched him. There was no friendliness coming from them as he'd felt from the trees in Central Park. Here was a waiting, brooding atmosphere.

Gradually Charley adapts to these Blue Ridge Mountains and learns to appreciate the sometimes ornery, always self-reliant folk who live in them. The setting, in fact, lies at the heart of the story, maturing him as well as determining ensuing events, and the reader cannot jump over the parts that deal with it without losing the thread of what is going on.

Equally involving settings can be created entirely out of the author's imagination as long as enough detail is supplied to allow the reader to share the picture. For example, in the genre of science fiction, *The Boy Who Reversed Himself* by William Sleator suggests the existence of an alternative world of four dimensions, explaining it so logically that by the end of the story a fourth dimension seems a plausible concept. "Four-space," as the characters call it, bisects "three-space" at right angles, and in it one can see the inside as well as the outside of objects. Laura is introduced to this bizarre place by Omar, a boy who has just moved in next door, and here is her description of what she sees on one of her first visits:

> We landed. The movement stopped. The light fixture, which usually hung from the ceiling, now stuck out horizontally from the right, the little bugs still crawling around inside it. Omar hung between me and the light. His features were all pushed over to one side, like a modern painting in which you see the profile and the front view at the same time. A large part of what should have been his head was a mass of dark purple, penetrated by two sharp little beams of light.
>
> "Omar," I whispered. "I think I'm looking inside your head."

What starts out for Laura as fascinating exploration turns into terrifying entrapment when she is accidentally lost in four-space without her experienced guide. Though totally invented, the setting is described as specifically as any mountainside or seashore, and it dominates the story, revealing the character of those trying to escape from it and presenting them with ever-increasing danger.

Frequently setting is a primary element in fantasy/science fiction, for the genre specializes in the depiction of strange places that need to be developed at length if they are to believed. But there are other kinds of stories also in which setting is crucial to the narrative, and many beloved children's books are found in these categories. Survival tales, for example, are very dependent on setting, for it becomes the antagonist in conflict with the character or characters caught in the predicament.

A classic of this type, based on a historical incident, is the novel *Island of the Blue Dolphins* by Scott O'Dell, winner of the 1960 Newbery Medal and later adapted into a well-received movie. In it, the Indian girl Karana is stranded on her home island off the coast of California when the villagers hurriedly leave to seek refuge from hostile, otter-hunting Aleuts. At first, Karana expects that they will return for her, but gradually she gives up hope of rescue and decides to leave the village for a safer location on a rocky headland.

> It was a morning of thick fog and the sound of far-off waves breaking on the shore. I had never noticed before how silent the village was. Fog crept in and out of the empty huts. It made shapes as it drifted and they reminded me of all the people who were dead and those who were gone. The noise of the surf seemed to be their voices speaking.

She then methodically burns each hut in the village, erasing her memories and preparing herself for a life alone that lasts eighteen years. Except for one brief interlude, there are no other human characters in the story, but the setting of the island, its plants and animals, provides the author with ample drama for a moving, fast-paced tale of adventure.

Setting is also important in regional fiction that portrays the people and customs typical of a particular area. An example I recall from the Morrow list is a Maine author named Elizabeth Ladd, who wrote a number of middle grade stories about children growing up on an island reached only by ferry, much like her native Islesboro. True to her frugal New England nature, she submitted her first manuscript single-spaced on both sides of the sheet, and it sat on the reading pile for many extra days because it looked both so daunting and unpromising to read. Finally one of the staff picked it up, prepared to give it a cursory look, but found herself instead drawn into a vividly evoked picture of farm life on coastal

Maine. Other readers were equally taken with it, and the following year Morrow published it under the title of *Enchanted Island*, the editors never quite getting over their surprise that a real writer could be discovered buried in such an unprofessional-looking manuscript. On this one occasion, strength of setting had triumphed over weakness of presentation, but in today's more competitive climate I suspect this self-taught talent might never come to light.

Because it is concerned with other times and other places, historical fiction is still another genre that often features interesting and colorful settings. The author brings the past to life by showing the surroundings in which the characters move, whether simply for younger readers or at greater length for older. *Sarah, Plain and Tall* by Patricia MacLachlan, for instance, takes place during the American pioneer days of the last century, and the story turns on a conflict between two settings: the prairie and the sea. The children Anna and Caleb long for a mother who will sing around the home as their own did before she died, and when Sarah answers Papa's ad for a wife, they are filled with hope. She arrives for a trial visit when the prairie is at its best.

> Sarah came in the spring. She came through green grass fields that bloomed with Indian paintbrush, red and orange, and blue-eyed grass.

But Sarah has lived all her life with her brother, William, in Maine, and she misses the sea. The children wince every time she speaks of it, for they are sure she is going to leave them for her beloved home.

> "In Maine," said Sarah, "there are rock cliffs that rise up at the edge of the sea. And there are hills covered with pine and spruce trees, green with needles. But William and I found a sand dune all our own. It was soft and sparkling with bits of mica, and when we were little we would slide down the dune into the water."
>
> Caleb looked out the window.
>
> "We have no dunes here," he said.

In the end, Sarah makes her choice between the prairie and the sea, telling Anna and Caleb that she would miss them more than her old home. The relationship of the characters to the setting forms the core of the story, enabling the author to dramatize in concrete images their need for love. Widely admired for its combination of emotional power and simplicity, *Sarah, Plain and Tall* was awarded the Newbery Medal in 1985, even though this honor usually goes to more complex novels.

Setting, characterization, plot. All three elements are needed to give a narrative pace and variety, but frequently setting is overlooked. To guard against the omission, writers should make it part of their advance planning and then continue to visualize each scene once the actual writing begins. Background gives the reader something to look at, establishes atmosphere, and helps to make a story emotionally strong.

4

The Dialogue

An ingenious, self-confident boy, who always has a pet project and plenty of friends to help him with it. A smart, impulsive girl, who sometimes gets into trouble because she is inclined to act without thinking. A timid child, who is shy with strangers and uncomfortable away from home. A flippant city teenager, used to danger in the streets and skilled in the art of survival. Put these characters into a story, and they will have to speak differently, according to their age and personality, if they are going to be believable. In fact, the dialogue written for them is the primary way, along with action and unspoken thoughts, that the author develops their characterization, the second major element of narrative.

Although beginners are apt to neglect the setting of their story, they frequently do the opposite with dialogue and overemphasize it. For many, telling what is happening by letting two characters talk about it is easier than gathering the information needed to describe a piece of action or the background in detail. If two girls are playing tennis, for example, a writer can avoid the need to learn the names of strokes, game strategies, even how to score by focusing instead on what they say to each other across the net or when they leave the court for home. But then the incident loses conviction, the scene becomes colorless, and the story begins to seem boring.

Actually nothing is quite so dull as an extended conversation between two characters without any pauses for action or description. Talking heads are no more interesting in a book than they are on a television screen or in a movie. As a young editor, I quickly picked up the reader's technique of scanning manuscripts for quotation marks. If I saw that every paragraph for two or three pages in a row began with them, I was alerted to a monotonous style and could then simply spot check to find out whether the initial impression was borne out or not. In the office, the staff referred to these submissions as "conversation pieces," a designation that usually meant no further consideration was necessary. Stories in which dialogue dominates action and visualization, or any single element overbalances the others, almost always lack the pacing needed to sustain reader interest.

Nevertheless, even though it must be kept under control, speech is an essential part of storytelling, bringing immediacy to a scene and revealing character. For one thing, it suggests how old a young person is, and writers for children spend considerable time matching vocabulary with the age of the child being portrayed. Over and over students discuss whether the girl in someone's story talks like an eight-year-old or whether the toddler in another could possibly know such a long word at age three. They are right to be concerned too, for nothing punctures the plausibility of a children's story quite so fast as a youngster speaking in the formal phrases that a middle-aged teacher might use, for example. Obviously the writer has written the dialogue in his or her own voice and has not been able to make that leap in point of view from adult to child that marks the successful juvenile author.

Because the speech of children changes so rapidly from one year to the next, answering questions about appropriate dialogue for a particular age is never easy. Usually there is wide disagreement when the use of a specific word or phrase is debated, depending on how recent and widespread the person's contact with young people is. The more I've listened to these discussions, however, the more I've come to feel that writers should not get bogged down in the fine points of word choice but, within common sense limits, think more in terms of point of view. If the attitude expressed in a conversation is believably childlike, then the individual words are likely to seem fitting. Children vary too much in their capabilities to make overly precise generalizations useful.

How fictional characters speak also can tell the reader something about their family background and where they have lived. Children growing up in the American South will not express themselves in the same way as those from New England. A Native American boy on a Navajo reservation in Arizona or a Chinese girl in San Francisco's Chinatown will probably talk differently from an Iowan farm youngster. But writers must be careful not to exaggerate these differences by repeating the same words over and over or by using difficult dialect spellings. Repetition can become an irritation, and oddly spelled words can make a conversation hard to follow, especially for young people who are still in the throes of developing their reading skills. Again control of dialogue is essential.

Most of all speech reveals the personality of a character to the reader. Is a child glib or inarticulate, aggressive or withdrawn? The writer must have the particular traits of the person in mind when writing dialogue for him or her and keep them consistent throughout the story. Change can occur, and is necessary for a plot, but when it comes, there must be a reason for it. When a fearful boy, for instance, answers the school bully back for the first time, something must happen to give him the courage: karate lessons, the help of a friend, or whatever.

A common pitfall that beginners should guard against when writing for children is using dialogue to convey the author's point of view instead of the character's. A temptation to those who want to improve their young readers, this short cut usually results in a story that either preaches or instructs; in any case, it sounds false. An example from my files is the following conversation that two boys have in an unpublished novel intended for teenagers about the dangers of drug addiction.

> "If Sandy hadn't messed with drugs, she'd still be alive."
> "Well, it won't ever happen to me," Tommy answered.
> "I'm sure Sandy thought it would never happen to her."
> "I guess you're right. After all, a lot of famous people have overdosed—Janis Joplin, Jimmy Hendrix [sic]."
> "Don't forget Elvis Presley and Sid Vicious, too."

These characters do not sound like high schoolers but like an adult with a message for them, so the story immediately loses credibility. In an editorial office, this kind of mismatching of voice to person is a weakness that manuscript readers seem to notice before any other.

Re-creating communication between characters is not the only function of dialogue; it can also be used to further the other storytelling elements. For example, the writer can advance the action in a scene by including a comment from a character on what is happening at intervals. The tennis match that was boring to read about because it was all talk would be equally dull if it were all motion. When it is described with a combination of dialogue *and* action, however, then it becomes livelier and more interesting. The mixture of an angry verbal exchange over a line call with a specific play that the author has invented to cause trouble is a surer way to create drama than relying on either the remarks or the behavior alone.

Similarly the writer can flesh out the description of a setting by having characters make observations about it to each other. In the science fiction novel *This Time of Darkness* by H.M. Hoover, a boy named Axel and a girl named Amy escape from their fetid subterranean city to one with a view of blue sky and sun. Only Axel has previously known such miracles, and he needs to explain what they see to Amy.

> "Amy, come over here," Axel called softly, and when she came, he pointed down a long hall where people walked. In the distance were more trees; beyond them was a stretch

of blue. "That looks like a park . . . you don't know what that is, but I think we can see out from there—maybe all the way to the ground!"

As the children explore the wonders of this new place, the author interweaves her picture of it with the conversation of the children about it, giving the story pace and variety.

Dialogue can serve additional purposes in storytelling too, and calling on these techniques will enrich the writer's style. For instance, spoken words can act as a counterpoint, sometimes humorous, other times serious, to what a character may be thinking in a scene. An exercise that demonstrates the value of this device is to write 500 words that contrast how a character talks with how he feels in a situation of conflict. You might portray, for example, a child under parental pressure to put up with the unwelcome attentions of a visiting relative, a young boy trying to speak politely, though wincing inside, as an effusive aunt pinches his cheek. Or you might try to show a child putting on a brave face while going through a fearful experience such as encountering a sudden wind and rain squall during a sailboat outing.

One student used this kind of counterpoint to amusing effect in a story about a family's involvement with Little League baseball. It tells of a boy whose father becomes coach of his team and how he is continually embarrassed, though he tries to hide his chagrin, by his father's old-fashioned boyish enthusiasm. Among other gaffes, the father habitually whistles "Take Me Out to the Ballgame" when taking the team to the ball field, and things just get worse as the season progresses.

Another helpful technique is to use dialogue to replace a flashback when the writer needs to let the reader know about something that has happened before the story opens. Under any circumstances, the time transitions of flashbacks, from the present to the past and back again, require a great deal of skill to manage smoothly. When writing for children, they become even more of a problem as readers will have had less experience following a narrative that jumps around in time. I still remember Jean Lee Latham's telling the audience in her Newbery Medal acceptance speech for *Carry on, Mr. Bowditch*, a biography of navigator Nathaniel Bowditch, that she had given the manuscript to a neighboring child to read, asking her to identify the boring parts. When the young reader reported back, the passages she had listed for Latham were without exception flashbacks that apparently were difficult to follow. So Latham rewrote them, narrating events in chronological order instead, and solved the problem. More than an interesting anecdote, this experience contains good advice for the juvenile writer.

In *Sarah, Plain and Tall*, the mother has died a number of years before the story opens, so Patricia MacLachlan cannot dramatize it in immediate action. Possibly she could have recalled it in a flashback, but instead she reveals it in the following conversation that Caleb starts while his sister, Anna, is baking bread:

"What did I look like when I was born?"

"You didn't have any clothes on," I told him.

"I know that," he said.

"You looked like this." I held the bread dough up in a round pale ball.

"I had hair," said Caleb seriously.

"Not enough to talk about," I said.

"And she named me Caleb," he went on, filling in the old familiar story.

"I would have named you Troublesome," I said, making Caleb smile.

"And Mama handed me to you in the yellow blanket and said . . ." He waited for me to finish the story. "And said . . . ?"

I sighed. "And Mama said, 'Isn't he beautiful, Anna?' "

"And I was," Caleb finished.

Caleb thought the story was over, and I didn't tell him what I had really thought. He was homely and plain, and he had a terrible holler and a horrid smell. But these were not the worst of him. Mama died the next morning. That was the worst thing about Caleb.

"Isn't he beautiful, Anna?" Her last words to me. I had gone to bed thinking how wretched he looked. And I forgot to say good night.

Here is a classic example of dialogue replacing a flashback in order to make the reader feel the poignancy of a past event more directly and to keep a narrative as simple and tight as possible.

Still a further use of dialogue is to show what the secondary characters may be thinking and feeling in a situation. The writer can relate the thoughts of the primary, or viewpoint, character, but cannot enter the mind of others at the same time without making the scene seem artificial and manipulated. Just as an actual person must intuit the attitude of another from speech, expression, and gesture, so must the reader, through the eyes and ears of the fictional protagonist, decide what the rest of the cast is thinking from external signals, mainly words uttered.

The central character in the middle grade story *Aldo Applesauce* by Johanna Hurwitz is a nine-year-old boy who becomes a vegetarian because he loves animals so much. The family has newly moved to the suburbs from the city, and now Aldo Sossi has many more animals to observe and care for, including all the birds in the backyard. When he sees how avidly the birds feed on the bread crusts that he throws out for them, he asks his mother for more.

"Enough is enough," argued Mrs. Sossi. "I have to worry about feeding our family and the cats. I can't assume responsibility for all the birds in the neighborhood too."

Aldo looked in the refrigerator and found a dish containing some leftover spaghetti from three nights before. "Is anyone going to eat this?" he asked.

"I doubt it," said his mother.

"Then I'll give it to the birds," said Aldo triumphantly. "They'll think it's a new kind of worm."

"Aldo is trying to make vegetarians out of the sparrows," Mrs. Sossi observed to her husband as he walked into the kitchen.

Not only is the mother's remark to Aldo's father amusing, it reveals to me something about her attitude toward her son's vegetarianism: respect for his belief, but a certain weary resignation with having to cope with it from day to day. The dialogue the author writes for this secondary character gives the reader an idea of what she is thinking, although her actual thoughts never appear in the narrative.

Since children are in the process of learning how to use words, they make mistakes that lead to a conversational misunderstanding from time to time. This universal experience of childhood gives juvenile writers much material for word play in dialogue, and examples abound in children's literature. Sometimes they are humorous, at other times upsetting, but all add a certain suspense to the narrative until the confusion is resolved. One often quoted example occurs in the opening chapter of *Ramona the Pest* by Beverly Cleary. During her first day of kindergarten, the irrepressible Ramona is told by her teacher to sit down for the present. Hardly able to believe her good fortune, Ramona sits down instantly and is very, very quiet for the rest of class. But the present Ramona is expecting never comes, and to her intense disappointment she learns her first school lesson: the word *present* does not always mean *gift*.

Another particularly sobering example came to me from a mother who recalled a misunderstanding that arose when her son was in first grade. He arrived home on a spring afternoon, announcing firmly that he didn't want to go to school the next day. At first, he wouldn't say why, but after his mother pressed him he finally told her because he was going to die. She tried to convince him that he was wrong, but nothing would shake his conviction, so at last she managed to reach the teacher by phone and find out what had happened to give him this idea. Easter was approaching, and the teacher had planned a class activity of dyeing eggs to celebrate the holiday, warning the students that they were going to dye tomorrow so they would wear appropriate clothes. The boy had never dyed eggs before, the custom did not exist in his culture, so in retrospect his confusion was understandable, but it took the adults by surprise at the time. Happily it left no ill effect, yet it still seemed a hard way to learn the difference between *die* and *dye*.

Interestingly, many cite phrases from the Pledge of Allegiance when they recollect words that they misinterpreted while being taught them in school. Several years ago playwright Arthur Miller wrote a piece in opposition to learning by rote for the Op Ed page of the *New York Times*, in which he referred to his amusingly distorted boyhood version of the Pledge. It is an apt demonstration of the mix-ups over words that can occur in childhood and shows the importance of listening carefully to the words that children are actually using in their speech. Miller says:

> Dirigibles were much in the news, in the early 20's, and the Navy, as far as I was able to make out, owned them. Thus, the patriotic connection, which was helped along by the fact that nobody I had ever heard speaking English had ever used the word Indivisible. Or Divisible either, for that matter.
>
> None of which inhibited me from rapping out the Pledge each and every morning: ". . . One Nation in a Dirigible, with Liberty and Justice for All." I could actually see in my mind's eye hordes of faces looking down at Earth through the windows of the Navy's airships. The whole United States was up there, all for one and one for all—and the whole gang in that Dirigible. One day, maybe I could get to ride in it, too, for I was deeply patriotic, and the height of Americanism, as I then understood it, was to ride in a Dirigible.

Opportunities for word play crop up constantly, and beginning writers should be on the alert for them, keeping a notebook of the interesting possibilities that they hear. Verbal confusions, like a child singing of *bandaids* on the knee instead of *banjos*, as one author reported to me, sometimes provide just the touch needed to liven up a fictional conversation.

Not all juvenile authors have the advantage of daily contact with children, so they seek it out in other ways. Some have told me that they make a habit of going to the nearby shopping mall, for instance, where they can listen in on the banter of the young people who congregate there. Whatever the technique, writers need to develop an ear for the way people talk and become skilled in reproducing what they hear on paper. A helpful exercise to begin might be to see if you can establish in a two-page conversation that one speaker is eight years old and the other is four, without stating their ages directly. Another is to write two pages of dialogue for a first-person narrative, in which the gender of the narrator is revealed through his or her speech alone. The aim is to be able to produce distinct voices that ring true and will not be confused with each other during the course of a story.

A prime concern of the writer when creating dialogue is to make absolutely clear who is speaking, and here mastering a few simple rules of technical presentation can be extremely useful. The first is to remember that only one speaker appears in a paragraph; when the speaker changes, you start a new paragraph, which is a visual clue for the reader. The word *said*, of course, is the standard link between speech and person, but some beginners worry about repeating it too much and strain for a substitute. Elaborate variations can be intrusive, however, and since *said* remains in the background anyway, usually the better practice is to call on it whenever it seems natural.

Another way of identifying the speaker is to give the person a gesture or piece of action—some stage business—either before or after the words uttered. In fact, doing so will have the added benefit of contributing motion to what otherwise might be a static scene. Paula Danziger, a widely read author of teenage stories known for her snappy dialogue, makes good use of this device. In *The Cat Ate My Gymsuit*, ninth-grader Marcy has the following argument with her father over the dismissal of her favorite teacher:

> My father started. "I suppose you are impressed by this woman's actions."
> "I've learned a lot in her class."
> He slammed down his coffee cup. "I want you to stay out of this, Marcy. You are not going to turn into a revolutionary. Learn to play by the rules."
> I concentrated on pouring the milk on my cornflakes.
> My mother put her hand on mine. "I'm sorry. I was very impressed by her when I met her at the PTA meeting."
> I asked, "Can I go to the hearing?"
> "Martin. Why don't we go together—you and me and Marcy. I know it's important to her."

There are three people in this breakfast-table conversation, but though the speakers change rapidly, their voices stay distinct. By means of stage business, addressing another by name, and expressing strong opinions, the author keeps them separate from each other. Her control of their identity is largely responsible for the fast pace of the dialogue, for the reader never has to pause to figure out who is saying what.

A writer equally skilled with this kind of breezy, rapid-fire conversational style is Avi, and his story *Romeo and Juliet Together (and Alive!) at Last* is an excellent example of how to control dialogue. The plot concerns the comic misadventures of an independent student production of *Romeo and Juliet*, requiring much talk both on and off stage. In less practiced hands, the long passages of uninterrupted banter might pall, but Avi brings them off with élan by consistently matching speech to personality.

Sometimes writers underline the identity of a speaker by giving the character a frequently recurring pet expression. In the Newbery-winning story *From the Mixed-Up Files of Mrs. Basil E. Frankweiler* by E.L. Konigsburg, there are two major characters: Claudia, age twelve, and her brother Jamie, age nine. When Claudia reveals her plan for them to run away from home and live in the Metropolitan Museum of Art, she wins Jamie over quickly because, as he says, "I like complications." This phrase then becomes a refrain that both marks Jamie's dialogue and demonstrates his adventurous spirit.

Marian Potter uses the same technique to personalize the speech of Maureen McCracken, protagonist of *A Chance Wild Apple*. In sixth grade, Maureen is studying percent, which she considers a great improvement over fractions, and she likes to insert percentage estimates into her conversation whenever possible. While picking up mail at the rural post office in the Ozarks with her younger brother, Walter, she lingers to chat cozily with the postmistress about the canning that she is helping with at home.

> Walter, ready to leave, tugged impatiently at Maureen's hand, but she wanted to try using percent. "I'd say we have 82 percent of our canning done. Just about everything but apple butter. We're doing that tomorrow."

The mature sound of this impromptu arithmetic pleases Maureen so much that she begins to convert all kinds of information, no matter how unlikely, into percentages, and the mannerism becomes a humorous leitmotiv running through her dialogue. It not only adds color to the way she talks, it tells the reader something about her personality: gregarious, bright, and a bit of a show-off.

Some writers turn to slang expressions for material that will individualize the speech of youthful characters, but my advice is to use them sparingly. As a rule, children's books stay in print longer than adult books, so authors, particularly of contemporary stories, should look for language that will sound current for as long as possible. This year's slang, however, may be passé by the next and then will produce the opposite effect. The "in" phrase may soon outdate a story and shorten its life unnecessarily instead of giving it a lasting, authentic ring. A safer technique is to create child appeal in the point of view of the characters, not in the fads of their vocabulary.

Good dialogue is primarily accomplished with control and contrast. The storyteller does not let it overbalance the other narrative elements of setting and action but uses it in combination with them to achieve variety and pace. Characters express themselves in different ways so that the speech of one can never be confused with that of another, and the reader never has to return to the beginning of a conversation to check off who has the floor for a key remark. Just as writers need to develop an observant eye for details that will make descriptions vivid, so they must have an attentive ear for language that will bring fictional characters to life. The voices in a story should not sound like the author's but have a distinct identity that emerges naturally from age, background, and personality.

5

The Characters

The budding entrepreneur, the eager-to-please show-off, the irritating crybaby, the aggressive street fighter. Not only will they speak differently when they appear in a story, they will act and think differently. One may be the first to raise her hand when the classroom teacher asks a question while another shrinks into his seat, preoccupied with thoughts of how to deal with the school bully on the way home. The toddler may hide behind his father's legs whenever he meets an unfamiliar grown-up while the young business woman doesn't hesitate to introduce herself to strangers, especially if she senses a job opportunity in the offing. To create a full characterization, the writer blends speech, unspoken thoughts, and action together, exploring amusing or touching contrasts that make up an individual personality.

The key to developing believable characters is the ability to provide convincing motivation for their behavior, whether it is helpful or destructive, consistent or contradictory. Writers need to be curious rather than judgmental about why someone acts in a surprising way and then translate this attitude into the handling of their fictional people. As an example, imagine that a driver in another car suddenly appears and takes a parking space you have been patiently waiting for. Nonwriters can simply get mad and look for a way to express their outrage, but you must try to train yourself to figure out a reason for this social theft. Is the driver late for an important

appointment, upset by a domestic argument, or too unobserv-
ant to be aware of others? Whatever, the author must be able
to view a conflict from several points of view in order to
understand all the people involved in it and make them
credible.

Before starting the actual narrative, the writer should have
a complete picture of the protagonist in mind, and for many
the first step is finding an appropriate name. It must have the
right national or ethnic flavor, sometimes it must be typical of
a particular time period, and it must contrast well with the
names of the rest of the characters. A good practice is to make
a note of intriguing names that one encounters in everyday
life, which is how the author Johanna Hurwitz discovered the
name of Bolivia for the girl in her story *Hot and Cold Summer*.
While appearing in the booth of her publisher at the inaugural
"New York Is Book Country" street fair, she met a young
Bolivia and, struck by the name, mentally filed it away for use
in a story someday. A few years later, when writing about a
new group of characters, Johanna not only had a name for the
visiting girl at hand, she had a reason that would explain her
presence on the scene for the whole summer; of course, she
must be the daughter of anthropologists, staying with her
relatives while her parents were away on a trip to a site in
South America.

Other authors report that they consult the telephone
directory when christening a new character. How much time
some spend creating a personality before they begin to write
is described well in the following excerpt from a *New York
Times Magazine* profile of Georges Simenon, the late Belgian
mystery writer:

> "You know what I still have somewhere?" [Simenon]
> says with enthusiasm. "My telephone books from every
> town in America and every big city in the world. Because
> when I need a name for a character, I take the book from
> the region—Boston, for example, or Salzburg, and I write
> the name on a manila envelope. Then I put down everything
> about him; his teachers, his grandmother, his telephone

number, and so on. I won't use these details in my novel, but I need to know everything about the man or woman who will be my character."

Many find that taking the time to develop such advance warm-up sketches of the major characters in a story is extremely helpful, and the information that they compile about them can be extensive. One author-teacher, whom I heard speak at a South Carolina writers' conference I participated in, suggested that imagining what kind of underwear a fictional person is wearing is an excellent way to get to know him or her inside out both literally and figuratively. To give yourself experience with this technique, start by writing about a character in a situation of conflict using five different techniques, 100 words for each: narrative, action, dialogue, unspoken thoughts, and the thoughts of a secondary character. The exercise is designed to make writers aware of which narrative form they are using and to lead them to flesh out their characterization as much as possible.

In one such exercise, a student chose for her subject a teenage girl distraught over a pimple that has just appeared on her face. First, in the narrative section, she introduced the girl examining her face in the bathroom mirror and explained why she is upset. Next she described the actions that the girl takes to get rid of the pimple and her increasing frustration as nothing proves effective. At that point, she brought the mother into the scene and created a dialogue between the two about whether the problem is worth all the girl's anguish. She then revealed the girl's private worries, carefully concealed from the mother, about the impression she will make on an upcoming date. Finally she offered the mother's tart thoughts about the excitability of adolescent girls and her hope that this stage would pass soon. By using these five writing tools, the writer had produced two convincing characters with a relationship that promised story possibilities out of a prosaic family encounter.

If you were to incorporate this incident into a story,

however, you would not be able to use all the material. Probably you would be limited by the point of view of the narration to the thoughts of only one character, and you wouldn't need some of the introductory, explanatory detail either. Instead, you should think of the exercise as a warm-up that will help you develop characters fully and ready them for the plotting to come. One student was working on a mystery about a boy who exposes a scheme to steal exotic birds from a pet shop, but she was having trouble making the ringleader credible. So she put him through the paces of the exercise, writing about him in five paragraphs of narration, action, dialogue, unspoken thoughts, and the thoughts of the pet-store owner. By the end, she not only had a clear grasp of how he spoke, acted, and thought, she knew the reasons for his behavior and was much more comfortable writing about him.

A helpful concept to remember when developing characters for a story is that, as in real life, they should exhibit a mosaic of overlapping, sometimes contradictory traits. The bright child may lack discipline and so have surprising difficulty achieving goals. The sympathetic person may have a rebellious streak and so get along with the needy but pick fights with the powerful. Characters representing one trait only—selfishness, greed, belligerence, or whatever—usually seem manipulated by the writer to demonstrate an idea and emerge as lifeless stick figures.

Memorable fictional characters are multifaceted, and one example among many in children's literature is Anastasia Krupnik, heroine of a half-dozen or more titles by Lois Lowry. Precocious because she is so articulate for her pre-adolescent age, Anastasia sometimes causes havoc in the adult world with her all-too-honest pronouncements. Her view of events, like that of most young people, is self-centered, and yet she is too intelligent not to learn from others. At the conclusion of the first book about her, *Anastasia Krupnik*, she informs her parents solemnly that she has a "mercurial temperament"; indeed, she is a true "mosaic of traits," full of surprises but always remaining in character even when changing her mind.

In this story, Anastasia must adjust to the shocking news that her mother has become pregnant without consulting her. The second book in the series, *Anastasia Again!*, opens with a scene in which her parents tell her of another stunning event to come:

> "The suburbs!" said Anastasia. "We're moving to the suburbs? I can't believe it. I can't believe that you would actually do such a thing to me. I'm going to kill myself. As soon as I finish this chocolate pudding, I'm going to jump out the window."
>
> "We live on the first floor," her mother reminded her.

By this time, the baby brother, Sam, is two and a half, and already his personality is just as individual as Anastasia's. Perhaps due to the influence of the father, who is an English professor at Harvard, Sam is also extremely verbal as Lowry amusingly demonstrates.

> Sam had *never* said ma-ma or da-da or by-by. He had started talking like Walter Cronkite before he was a year old. Anastasia's mother *swore* that one day when he was four months old, he had said, "Thank you," when she fed him some strained apricots; but no one believed her, and she had no witnesses.

The two children are allies now, and though they originally try to derail the move to the country, they settle in quickly and dominate their new surroundings as easily as their old.

Choosing an appealing central character like Anastasia for a story can be all important, and there are several helpful factors to keep in mind when doing so. For one thing, the age of the child must be appropriate for the situations that will figure in the plot, and this matching takes careful thought as capabilities in addition to speech change rapidly in childhood. One example that comes to mind is a student's middle grade

novel about an eight-year-old girl trying to become independent of her eleven-year-old brother. An early crisis between
the two concerned the first time the parents leave them alone
for a few hours on a Saturday morning without a baby sitter
and the girl's feelings of outrage when the boy is officially put
in charge. For the reader to be sympathetic with her and her
dilemma, her age must be just right. If she is too young, her
resentment will seem uncalled for; if she is too old, the
problem will seem unlikely to have arisen in the first place.
Interestingly, the ages of the children seemed on target for
this scene, but the attitude of the parents toward them did
not. They were portrayed as being extremely anxious about
the occasion and all too aware of why the girl might be
unhappy about it. If the writer showed them as less percep-
tive, however, then the girl would have more reason to feel
misunderstood, and the tensions would be strengthened.
Clearly a key factor in the credibility of the story was going
to be what *all* the characters thought was appropriate behavior
for an eight-year-old.

Another requirement for an effective central character is
giving him or her a dramatic conflict of one type or another.
Although the possibilities are endless, they can be grouped
into four basic categories—with self, with another person,
with a social group, with the environment—and children's
literature offers numerous excellent examples of each. For a
character in conflict with self, the emotionally wrenching
story *On My Honor* by Marion Dane Bauer, a 1987 Newbery
Honor Book, sets high standards. In it, the twelve-year-old
protagonist, Joel Bates, experiences an appalling tragedy when
his best friend, Tony, drowns while the two are swimming
alone together in the off-bounds, dangerous river that runs
outside their town. Although Joel was against the idea of the
swim, he blames himself for the accident and for being unable
to save Tony, and when he returns home, he cannot bring
himself to report what has happened. If only his father hadn't
given them permission to go off on their bicycles in the first
place. All afternoon Joel hides away in his room, and in the

evening he denies knowing anything about Tony's where-
abouts to the two sets of worried parents. Finally, however,
he blurts out the truth to them.

> Everybody was looking at him, blaming him. He
> wanted to turn away, to run at last, but his feet refused to
> carry him in that direction. Instead, he stumbled toward
> his father, his hands raised and clenched into fists. "I hate
> you!" he cried, pounding at his father's chest. "It's all your
> fault. You never should have let me go!"
>
> His father said nothing, did nothing to shield himself
> from Joel's fists. He simply stood there, absorbing the force
> of the blows until Joel could bear it no longer. He turned
> and leaped off the porch and bolted across the street.
>
> But even as he slammed through the door and ran up
> the stairs to his room, he knew. It wasn't his father he
> hated. It wasn't his father at all.
>
> He was the one. . . . Tony had died because of him.

The question that this plot poses is not whether Joel will
be punished or not—the reader knows his situation will be
understood—but whether he can resolve the conflict within
himself and stop blaming others for what has occurred. The
inner struggle is agonizing, and Joel's initial silence is shocking, yet he stays a sympathetic figure throughout, because the
reasons for what he says and does are ones that all can identify
with.

A similar self-conflict is the concern of a recently published first novel entitled *Eighty-Eight Steps to September*, which
earned widespread critical attention for newcomer Jan Marino. In this story, the eleven-year-old protagonist, Amy
Martin, refuses to come to terms with the reality that her
brother, Robbie, is dying of leukemia and requires hospitali-
zation. Resentful of the disruption caused by his illness,
convinced that her parents are exaggerating its severity, Amy
is a stubborn and uncooperative figure. Yet the reader never
stops rooting for her as she gropes her way toward an understanding of the situation and an easing of her own angry
turmoil.

Characters in conflict with others, the second type, are a staple of storytelling and turn up in narratives of all lengths including simple picture books. For example, the picture books about a ghost named Gus by Jane Thayer, the pseudonym author Catherine Woolley uses when writing for the very young, have remained popular for many years because of the strong characterizations in them. As indicated in the first title, *Gus Was a Friendly Ghost*, Gus himself is a gentle soul, but in contrast his friend Mouse has a terrible temper. When the summer folk return to reclaim the house the two have enjoyed during a cozy, isolated winter, Mouse is furious and starts a campaign to scare them away. He spills food, chews pillows, and stamps over their heads in the attic at night while the Scotts retaliate with artfully baited mousetraps. All Mouse succeeds in doing, however, is arousing Gus, who finally takes a strong hand and makes his feisty housemate behave himself. Despite his small size, Mouse is a character always ready to do battle, an apt foil for a peace-loving ghost and a creation colorful enough to help sustain another half-dozen or more stories.

The third kind of conflict, with the social group, is a constant concern of childhood, and so a fruitful source of material for juvenile literature. Among a number of stories about the oddball, shunned and tormented by classmates, is an especially powerful one by Marilyn Sachs entitled *The Bears' House*. She tells it from the point of view of the outcast, who introduces herself as follows:

> Everybody in my class knows my name.
> It's Fran Ellen Smith. I'm nearly ten. I suck my thumb, and everybody says I smell bad. (I can smell my smell. It's a sucking smell. I don't think it's bad. It smells like me.)

Fran Ellen has reason to suck her thumb, for she is one of five children, the youngest being seven months, with an absent father and a mentally ill mother. They have resolved to care for themselves to avoid being split up among different foster homes and must go to elaborate lengths to maintain the façade of a normal household. Fran Ellen's way of relieving the strain is to retreat from the world and enter into an ideal, imaginary life in the miniature Bears' House the teacher keeps in the back of the classroom. A spare and unsentimental portrait of a family situation out of control, the book does not offer easy solutions to Fran Ellen's conflict with society, but it does engender tremendous sympathy for the despised loner.

Another version of a similar conflict is presented in the 1989 Newbery Honor Book *Afternoon of the Elves* by Janet Taylor Lisle. This time the story is narrated by a nine-year-old friend of the troubled one, who is described at first as a "gaunt, fierce bird, a rather untidy bird if one took her clothes into consideration. They hung on her frame, an assortment of ill-fitting, wrinkly garments." But through the magical allure of the elf village Sara-Kate builds in her backyard, Hillary comes to admire her "wild and free" qualities and learn her secret: that she too is protecting an incompetent mother from an uncaring community whose help would only make matters worse.

> "Help is the last thing yo want to ask for when you're somebody like me," Sara-Kate told Hillary. "People like you can ask for help. People like me have to steal it."

Again the author does not attempt to provide a happy ending to this knotty problem; when at last the truth is discovered, Sara-Kate's mother is apparently "put someplace far way, out of sight," just as Sara-Kate had predicted. But Lisle does show that at times the individual—even an eleven-year-old child—has cause to be antagonistic toward society.

Finally, characters may find themselves in conflict with the environment, which has provided the theme for many stories of adventure and survival. A humorous and imaginative example, written for very young children, is Mary Calhoun's picture book *Cross-Country Cat*, about a smart Siamese named Henry, who finds himself abandoned in remote Western snow country. Realistic in its opening, the story shifts smoothly into fantasy as the cat dons a pair of toy skis, masters the "slide and glide" rhythm of the cross-country skier, and then braves such dangers as a threatening encounter with a marauding coyote. Like Henry, who has been a picture book favorite for many years, fictional animals or people who overcome external challenges make strong characters, satisfying to identify with at any age.

In fact, identification between the reader and the protagonist is important to establish no matter what kind of conflict he or she may be caught in. That process is needed to make a story credible, and it usually occurs when the fictional person emerges as a sympathetic figure whose behavior seems appropriate to the circumstances being unfolded by the plot. Beginners sometimes assume that a sympathetic central character means someone who always does the right thing, but actually the reverse is more often the case. The saintly one is frequently harder to identify with than someone who makes mistakes under duress. In *On My Honor*, Joel lacks the courage to tell the truth about the drowning, and the reader does not condemn him, because denial of the guilt he feels seems human. In *Afternoon of the Elves*, Sara-Kate steals food when her mother's money runs out, and readers still feel compassion for her, because they can imagine being driven to the same desperate measures in her situation. If sufficient motivation is provided for the error in judgment, then the character will gain, not lose, sympathy from the reader.

Successful heroes and heroines also tend to be strong characters with powerful drives and emotions that provide ample material for dramatic incidents. Making a shy, withdrawn person interesting is possible, but certainly much more difficult than working with a less inhibited personality. The ones that readers seem to take to heart most readily are the outsized personalities like Beverly Cleary's Ramona, who dares to squeeze out a whole tube of toothpaste when frustrated *(Ramona and Her Mother)*, or Katherine Paterson's embattled foster child Gilly Hopkins, who is happiest when she can fight six boys at once for possession of a basketball *(The Great Gilly Hopkins)*. So, when choosing a central character for a story, look for someone whose thoughts, speech, and behavior will have enough dimension to attract and hold the attention of an audience.

Although the writer may know the major characters well by the time he or she begins the actual narrative, the reader of course does not, which sometimes causes difficulties for beginners. I find that students often take their fictional people for granted and forget to include relevant detail about them, or they are in a rush to present all the background at once instead of revealing it gradually as events take place. In both these instances, I advise them to keep the widely repeated maxim of "show don't tell" in mind. For example, if a character is going to be portrayed as clumsy, the writer should resist taking the short cut of saying so when he first appears but rather invent a piece of behavior that will demonstrate this trait at an appropriate time.

In Marian Potter's novel *Blatherskite*, another in which Maureen McCracken of the Ozark Mountains is featured, she is characterized as a ten-year-old chatterbox, good-hearted but sometimes tiring. Then comes a scene in which Maureen's glib tongue saves the day, and it is a highlight because the author never intrudes her own voice; instead she *shows* the character in action by letting her do all the speaking. Caught accidentally on the crack express train to St. Louis with no tickets and no money to buy them, Maureen thinks quickly, blames the mishap on her younger brother, Walter, and talks the conductor into a free ride for both of them. Here is how she handles the conductor's second attempt to collect their tickets:

> Maureen's forced laugh sounded more like a grunt. "He finally told. I like to never got it out of him. He kept taking those tickets out of his pocket, taking them out, to see if he still had them. Then he put them in his mouth so's he would know he had them, and he got to chewing on them and got them all disgusting. And he thought I'd be mad, and he swallowed half of one and thought it wouldn't be

any good, so then he just threw the rest away as we got on the train."

The conductor gives up at this point, and the reader believes in his capitulation, because the author *shows* step-by-step rather than tells after the fact exactly how Maureen wears him down.

Crucial as a well-drawn central character is to the success of a story, however, writers should not overlook the importance of motivating the others in the cast—particularly those who are antagonists—just as carefully. Sometimes beginners are so eager to persuade a young audience of their sympathy that they take sides with the hero or heroine too strongly and give little consideration to anyone else. But the attitudes of the secondary players toward the lead provide the contrast that the writer must have to develop a fully rounded primary characterization. Whatever the plot conflict may be, more than one point of view about it needs to be convincingly expressed to make it interesting and generate suspense.

Two kinds of books that especially depend on a credible antagonist to make them believable are mysteries and adventure tales. If the villain responsible for the problem lacks adequate motivation, he or she becomes a cardboard figure and the plot becomes preposterous. Yet all too often writers seem so reluctant to expose young readers to evil that they cannot bring themselves to dramatize it with any conviction, and the project fails. A story about two boys lost in a Southwestern desert, threatened by frightening strangers, may be very exciting in its survival details, but if at the end the pursuers turn out to have no valid reason for their wrongdoing, it falls apart. Condemning destructive behavior as bad without explaining it is tempting for those who would like to improve children through their literature, but doing so does not produce memorable fiction.

Of course, secondary characters are not and should not be as fully developed as the primary characters. The writer does not try to create a sense of their inner, hidden self, but constructs them around a single idea, so that the reader is able to remember them easily, even though they are frequently off stage and removed from the action. In *Anastasia Again!*, for example, the baby brother, Sam, is identified with the one trait of precocious speech, and although he never surprises as a leading figure might by suddenly becoming tongue-tied, he still remains believable. He is what is known as a flat character while Anastasia is a round character, and both types are needed in a successful story.

True, when the author is able to make all the characters convincing, they may surprise their creator and take on a life of their own. I remember one such instance that happened in the course of publishing a teenage novel by Hila Colman entitled *Bride at Eighteen*. It concerned the stresses of marrying at a young age and the problems that can arise when the wife takes a job to put the husband through college. In one scene, she comes home from work to find to her dismay that he has gone to the beach with some classmates to celebrate the end of his school term instead of vacuuming the apartment as promised. The female editorial staff, apparently, identifying with the situation strongly, objected to his behavior far more than the author had anticipated and described the husband as selfish in the jacket copy prepared for the book. Hila thought the comment was inaccurate and tried to defend him—she had not intended to portray him as a heavy—but the character had become independent of *her* intentions, and she had to let him take the consequences for what had become *his* actions.

Just as a narrative needs to combine the three elements of description, dialogue, and action to become interesting, so a complete characterization should consist of thoughts, speech, and action. By mixing these three aspects together, the writer is able to show the contrasts in a character's personality: between what he says and does, between his intentions and achievements. The portrait should include faults as well as virtues, for both must be present to make the figure seem human, someone the reader can identify with. Then the fictional person comes alive on the page and brings credibility to the story.

6

The Plot

Will the baseball rookie make the team or be sent down to the minors? Will the refugee child, orphaned by war, escape from danger and find a home? Will the school newcomer win friends with his tall stories or end up in disgrace? Will the fat girl overcome her lack of confidence and learn to relax in the company of boys? These questions have all served as plots and provided a springboard for a sequence of events that first build and then resolve uncertainty about the outcome. Along with setting and characters, plot is an essential element in traditional storytelling and remains so in juvenile writing as young readers respond strongly to suspense and curiosity about what is going to happen next.

In a 1969 *New York Times Book Review* article decrying the lack of plot in modern fiction, the late Isaac Bashevis Singer called children's literature the last refuge of storytelling today. His point was that writers who wish to tell a story with a beginning, middle, and end now have more latitude to do so when writing for children than for adults, whose taste has turned to a naturalistic, slice-of-life style. For me, his observation rings true as, when I was an editor, I looked for stories with a definable structure, ones that posed a central question and at the end answered it. If I could sum up what a piece of fiction concerned in a few brief sentences, for colleagues, book reviewers, company salesmen, or whomever, then I felt it was more likely to appeal to the young.

So I stress to beginners the importance of plot in their work. It is a major narrative element, along with setting and characterization, and writers should keep all three in mind as they begin to shape the particular story that they want to tell, interrelating it with the people and places that it concerns. A helpful exercise to get started is to write 1,000 words about the child character that you have just finished developing, weaving together the strands of action, dialogue, and description in a single dramatic scene. For ideas, you might examine your own childhood and try to recall your unhappiest day or your most important decision. Some students question whether a child can make a truly important decision, but examples abound. For instance, I think of the person who reported that he made up his mind not to follow the religion of his parents at age ten, a choice that he felt changed the course of his life. Adults, especially those who want to write for children, sometimes need to remind themselves that young minds are serious as well as playful.

A theme for this exercise that lends itself to many variations is embarrassment or the shame of falling short of a goal. For example, a girl might forget her piece during a piano recital, but still save the performance with an amusing improvisation. Or a child might talk his father into taking him on a fishing trip, but make many mistakes before he finally brings in the catch of the day. In one that I recall, a student familiar with bloodhounds told of a boy who despairs of teaching his undisciplined puppy how to track until the dog meets the real challenge of finding a missing little girl. Whatever the subject, it should offer interesting possibilities for action, dialogue, and description, so that the writer can work on developing all three aspects of a scene and realize its full dramatic potential.

Before starting the narrative, however, a storyteller has several important decisions to consider in advance. An especially crucial one is which of the three possible points of view—single first person, single third person, or omniscient—to choose as, once adopted, it should be maintained consistently throughout. Many times an author does change his or her mind at some point in the plot about the most suitable viewpoint to use and goes back to the beginning to revise accordingly, but a little previous thought may help to avoid what can be a tedious process.

The advantage of the single first-person narrative voice is that it creates a full portrayal of the central personality and so enhances reader identification. For this reason, it has been popular with young adult writers, many of whom feel it is an effective way to show that they understand and sympathize with their audience. The disadvantage, though, is that it limits the ideas and impressions offered by the writer to those of the protagonist alone and so can make a story seem shallow and self-concerned. As a result, some reviewers have become tired of the style, one complimenting an author in *School Library Journal*, a magazine that reviews children's and young adult books, for using it without letting it become the familiar "recitation of grievances, delivered by a whining narrator of limited vocabulary and experience."

In fact, if the central character is strong enough, telling his or her story in first person can produce an original, one-of-a-kind effect. An example is the Richard Peck novel *Ghosts I Have Been*, which he narrates from heroine Blossom Culp's point of view. Blossom's voice has a leisurely, old-fashioned ring, which is appropriate as she is speaking in 1913, yet at the same time she is brisk and matter-of-fact about her status as an outsider. Here is the way she presents herself to the reader:

> There are girls in this town who pass their time upon their porches doing fancywork on embroidery hoops. You can also see them going about in surreys or on the back seats of autos with their mothers, paying calls in white gloves. They're all as alike as gingerbread figures in skirts. I was never one of them. My name is Blossom Culp, and I've always lived by my wits.

Daughter of a palmist with Gypsy blood in her veins, Blossom develops the powers of second sight during the course of the story and applies them with vigor and resourcefulness. Her crowning achievement is the discovery of a crime committed during the sinking of the *Titanic*, which leads to international fame and a presentation at the British Royal Court. The plot is a humorous send-up of Midwestern society after the turn of the century, and the decision to relate it in first person seems the right choice, for only Blossom has the larger-than-life presence that could succeed in suspending the reader's disbelief.

Because a first-person narration is primarily concerned with the motivations of a hero or heroine, it is often best suited to adventurous stories like *Ghosts I Have Been*, in which suspense is generated by someone's conflict with external circumstances. If the writer intends to explore subtleties in personal relationships, however, then the single third person may be a better choice. With this technique, a separation is created between the character and the narrator; they are not identical voices as in the first-person story. Unity of viewpoint is still maintained, so that the internal thoughts of secondary figures cannot be articulated, but nevertheless the author is able to hint at them indirectly by describing external gestures or facial expressions that the primary figure may not notice. Thus, the reader's knowledge of what is happening or anticipation of problems to come is not limited by what this single person knows and expects.

Juvenile writers need to be adept at slipping into another point of view, since they are almost never able to write directly from their own perspective, but must envision events as experienced by someone younger. Some of children's favorite books have been written by authors who carry this ability one step further and tell a story from a nonhuman viewpoint, such as that of an animal or inanimate object. In Beverly Cleary's story *Ralph S. Mouse*, for instance, the world is seen through the eyes of a mouse: sizes are in his proportion, information is geared to what he might reasonably understand. For this feat of imagination, she uses the single third-person viewpoint, which allows readers to identify with little Ralph even while they are placing his experiences in a larger context.

Cleary launches her plot with Ralph's decision to leave his home in a run-down hotel and find lodgings in the place that his human friend, Ryan, refers to as school. His understanding of "school," however, is necessarily incomplete, pieced together from fragments of conversation that he overhears in the lobby as guests come and go.

> To Ralph, school was a strange and mysterious place. When he had been a very young mouse, Ralph had pictured school as something like a bus, because mothers and fathers who arrived at the hotel with several children after a long, hot drive across the Sacramento Valley or the long, winding ride over the Sierra Nevada often said, "I'll be so glad when school starts." Ralph had naturally concluded that because a school started, it must also move like a car.

But some of Ralph's perceptions are universal and indirectly lead readers to look at themselves more objectively as when the mouse listens to the hotel manager scold the handyman for letting the lobby smell—well, mousey. "That's funny, thought Ralph. I can't smell a thing." Fair enough, are human smells really any less noticeable than mouse smells? Not as far as Ralph is concerned. The comment with its subtle comparison is just a brief aside, yet it shows how totally the author has been able to adopt another, quite different persona. At the same time, however, a more knowing narrator's voice speaks in the background, and the byplay between the two provides added amusement.

In stories told from the omniscient point of view, such as *The Girl Who Cried Flowers* by Jane Yolen, written in the tradition of the classic folktales, that narrator's voice is stronger than the voice of any single character. With the greater latitude of this technique, the writer can create several fully developed figures, either by viewing them externally or by moving the spotlight from one to another as the scene changes. Still to be avoided, however, are abrupt changes of internal point of view in the middle of a conversation or an exciting piece of action, since they are just as jarring in omniscient stories as in any other. More used in the past, especially for novels with a large cast of characters, the omniscient viewpoint rarely appears in contemporary juvenile writing, although modifications of the style show up in the work of some authors from time to time.

In *Lucie Babbidge's House* by Sylvia Cassedy, for example, the central figure is a girl who has retreated into an inventively detailed imaginary life after the trauma of losing her parents in a train accident. The author wants to keep the reader uncertain about where actuality ends and fantasy begins, to demonstrate how the line wavers in Lucie's mind, and she does so by relating the story from the vantage point of an outside observer who is not privy to everything that Lucie does. Early on Lucie, along with her classmates, receives a bean to plant as part of a botany lesson, and the observer reports that she draws two eyes and a mouth on it—"dot, dot, circle." But no connection is drawn between this action and the subsequent arrival of a new baby, whose eyes and mouth are described "dot, dot, circle," in Lucie's imaginary family. Only many chapters later, when Lucie's pot is the single one that does not sprout, does the reader begin to grasp that she never planted it but transformed it into an imaginary baby to play with instead. By distancing the narrator from the character, as is characteristic of the omniscient point of view, the author creates suspense and draws readers into the story by requiring them to make their own connections.

Another decision the writer should make in advance is what kind of conflict will lie at the heart of the plot and whether it is strong enough to energize everything that is going to happen. It can be internal, in which a character faces a self-created problem (a child adjusting to the arrival of a new baby in the family); external, in which a character is challenged by a person, group, or the environment (a mystery, an outdoor adventure); or a combination of internal and external, in which a character must struggle both with himself and outside forces. Usually the last option is the one that gives a story the most power and depth, and the work of the late juvenile sports novelist John R. Tunis is a classic example that comes to mind. His subjects concerned familiar themes of an athlete mastering the skills of track, baseball, basketball, etc., but to them he added social criticism of the circumstances in which the games are played, and in doing so transcended the form. The first to address such explosive issues as racism in baseball for the young, he dramatized in his plots both the internal pressures experienced by the player and the external pressures exerted by society. Books like *The Iron Duke, The Kid from Tomkinsville* and *Go, Team, Go!* immediately stood out from others in the genre and are still being read today.

Whatever type of conflict the writer chooses for his or her plot, it should never be a false one but always lead to a climax of some kind. Nothing is more disappointing for a reader than to discover that the problem presented by a plot is illusory, based on someone's lack of knowledge or misguided expectations. Sometimes beginners make the mistake of arbitrarily withholding information from a character in order to stretch out the suspense, as when a worried child waits till the last chapter, for no reason except the author's need, to ask her parents whether she is adopted or not. I can recall reading one such manuscript submission, and when the answer finally came, it hardly seemed worth the bother. Another instance of false conflict fatally flawed a promising story about a little Vietnamese girl who is evacuated during wartime to the United States for safety. Naturally she is terrified—of strange customs, of nonacceptance—but the author could not bring herself to portray such unkindness and instead gave her the warmest of welcomes in her new home, thus undermining all drama in the situation.

Another essential is that the conflict be central to the plot, of concern to the characters from the beginning to the end. If it is resolved too quickly, the rest of the story will inevitably become an anticlimax that cannot be rescued with the introduction of still further problems or still further people. Stringing a series of difficulties together is not an effective way to sustain plot momentum as the story then is likely to seem manipulated and lose credibility, like a daytime soap opera. So when deciding what your conflict is going to be, weigh carefully whether it has large enough scope, with sufficient ramifications, to support the entire storyline.

Lastly, after viewpoint and central conflict are established, you should consider in advance what the end of your plot is going to be, what point it is that you wish to make. How characters arrive at the final scene is often best left open, so the writer can take advantage of an unexpected idea that surfaces without warning while work is in progress, but most need to have an overall concept in mind to achieve narrative cohesion and drive. Does each incident contribute to the conclusion and maintain forward momentum, or are some a diversion that keeps everyone busy but has no bearing on the outcome? The writer who knows from the start the purpose of the story is able to judge more easily which possibilities to pursue and which may end up being pruned in a revision.

Sometimes beginners expect, or hope, that the initial draft of a story will be sufficient, that somehow they will be able to put all the elements together smoothly the first time around. But that feat is rare, and more often revision should be taken for granted, certainly nothing to be resisted. Shaping a narrative is usually a continuing process of improvement, involving simple adjustments like changing a character's name to avoid confusion with others or major ones like rethinking his motivation to make his behavior more credible.

A classic example of how extensively the best writers revise to perfect narrative flow and style is the work that E. B. White did on the first chapter of *Charlotte's Web*. All drafts of the manuscript have been preserved, so scholars and students have been able to look at the various arrangements of material and word choices that he tried out as he debated with himself what would make the strongest opening to the story. The main question appears to have been whether to begin with a description of the barnyard setting or with Fern's objections at breakfast when her father picks up his ax and leaves to kill the sickly runt in the sow's new litter. In the end, White chose dialogue over background, and the original chapter one was turned into chapter three, but clearly he was able to arrive at this decision only after the most lengthy and painstaking experimentation.

Of the authors I worked with, one who especially relied on revision was Carolyn Haywood. I knew how she went about it at first hand because she liked to have me read an upcoming project midway, so we could discuss any emerging problems early on. In particular, I remember the first draft of her story *Eddie's Happenings*, in which she introduced a character named Tookey Tully to her cast of regulars. A new boy in town, he quickly attracted attention because of the astounding claims that he made for himself and his family. These "whoppers," as Eddie called them, were fun but so obviously false that Tookey's reasons for telling them were unclear. After we talked about the lack of motivation, Haywood went back to her desk and came up with an original solution: Tookey was going to acquire an embarrassing lisp that he tried to compensate for with his outrageous tales. Of course, she had to revise the story from the beginning, rewriting every line of his dialogue to demonstrate the lisp, but she did so without hesitation, and this afterthought was just the touch needed to turn Tookey into a sympathetic and credible little boy.

Aspiring writers, however, rarely have the opportunity to confer with a professional book editor about a work in progress and must go to different sources for objective scrutiny of what they have put on paper. Workshops and critique groups can and do provide constructive interim feedback, and many participants gain additional insights from the experience of analyzing the efforts of others. But more times than not, the best writers prove to be those who are able to criticize themselves. This ability not only helps a writer begin publishing, by signaling when a manuscript is ready to be submitted, it protects the reputation of one who is established, indicating when a project is *not* working and should be filed away. A magazine writer named Sarah Juon expressed the need for self-criticism especially well in an article called "You're the Judge," which appeared in the November 1986 issue of *The Writer*. In it, she said, "The longer you've been writing, the more evident it becomes that you must become your own ideal reader." Her tips for achieving a neutral attitude toward one's work are *time* (rereading a piece when the emotions of creating it have faded) and *distraction* (working on something else to speed up disengagement).

Still, no matter how ready the writer is to revise, he or she should have some overall plot structure in mind when starting a story. One formula that many have found useful is "urge—barrier—struggle—resolution." It can take the form of showing how a person single-mindedly proceeds to accomplish a specific purpose, as in winning the election for class president, or how someone must make one or more difficult decisions in pursuit of the purpose, as whether to resort to underhanded campaign tactics or not. Usually the latter offers more scope for surprise and suspense, especially if the possible results of several courses of action are well laid out so that the reader feels pulled between them. For example, is the betrayal of a friend worth the office of president? In either case, the story begins with the primary character in a dilemma created by the barrier to the urge and then proceeds in a series of dramatic scenes as he or she takes steps to resolve it. For ideas of what this dilemma might be, imagine your character getting into trouble, making a mistake rather than doing the right thing. Perhaps the young presidential candidate has lost his temper in a public debate and said things about not allowing the girls to join boys' teams that he later regrets. Should he retract his words or brazen them out? The story tells of his struggle with this problem and ends with the outcome of his decision.

But how easily will that middle section of the plot, from the opening dilemma to the closing resolution, fall into place? Eve Bunting, both a teacher and a juvenile writer, says that more books are abandoned at this stage than at any other and describes how she overcomes "center sag" in an article called "Getting Through Those Miserable Middles" for the September/October 1984 issue of the newsletter of the Society of Children's Book Writers (SCBW). Her advice is to think in terms of three "despites" to the central question asked by the story. In other words, will the hero win the school election despite 1) his outspokenness, 2) opposition from the girls in the class, 3) his difficulty keeping his grades up with less time to study? By having three issues to develop, the writer is assured of enough material to provide a "strong foundation on which to build [the] plot."

Now that a basic structure is in place, the writer begins the actual narrative and turns his or her attention to making individual scenes as dramatic and suspenseful as possible. At first, thinking of a book scene like a stage scene may be helpful, and there is one important similarity in construction to keep in mind. Key pieces of action should take place center stage, not off stage and reported later, to give them immediacy for the reader. If a high point of the plot is going to be a school dance, and the characters have been looking forward to it for a number of chapters, don't skip over the evening and tell the reader about it the following week in a conversation or flashback. Surprisingly, that mistake of distancing the narrator from a major incident is more common than one might expect, almost as if the writer was afraid of not being able to make it worth the wait. However challenging, though, you should be sure to take full advantage of all the suspense that you have been able to generate and to describe each of your climaxes in full detail. These passages are your big dramatic opportunities and should not be wasted.

Of course, not every piece of action is equally important, and at times the writer needs to be able to incorporate background events indirectly into a plot without interrupting its flow. Flashbacks are the technique frequently used for this purpose, and a good rule of thumb is to consider them for incidents that occur before the story opens rather than for those that take place during its course. In an article entitled "In and Out of Flashbacks," published in the May 1986 issue of *The Writer*, author Margaret Hill discusses how the writer can keep the reader oriented as the narrative switches back and forth in time. She advises three devices: 1) using words and phrases such as "yesterday" and "on her fourteenth birthday" to signal a change; 2) controlling verb tenses carefully, so that the past perfect (*had* plus the verb) introduces a section that takes place earlier; 3) including concrete images such as a car or piece of furniture that can be repeated to bring the reader back to the current setting. When managed smoothly, flashbacks can help the writer unify material, but should never be used to replace a dramatic high point.

One element that automatically injects suspense into a scene is a time deadline of some kind. If a character has to catch a plane, turn in a school project by a certain date, or be ready for a set event to take place (packing for a vacation), the reader identifies and becomes tense about the outcome. In the 1971 Newbery-winning story *Summer of the Swans* by Betsy Byars, the heroine has to search for her retarded younger brother, who has wandered off during the night and lost himself in the woods. Clearly if she doesn't find him in a reasonable amount of time, he will come to great harm, and as the hours slowly pass the scene skillfully builds in its dramatic intensity. By describing the many small details of the search—what the girl sees, smells, hears—the author stretches out her narration of the incident to the maximum, making readers increasingly anxious as they wait for its resolution.

Nevertheless, important as the construction of each individual scene is, the writer must also keep in mind the overall construction of the story: how the scenes connect with each other. Plot has been defined as a sequence of events determined by cause and effect as well as linked together by time, meaning that each incident should lead convincingly to the next. The narrator is not just simply telling *what* happened next, but revealing *why* it happened, and in the process offering the reader some surprises. A plot that is entirely predictable is not very interesting, but of course the surprises need to be in character with the personalities of the people in the story, or they will not be believable. For instance, in *Summer of the Swans*, the plot does not merely turn on the disappearance of the retarded Charlie, but on *why* he wandered off, and the unexpected outcome lies in the sympathetic understanding that develops between his sister and a high-school boy while looking for him.

Pace is another key element that goes into the structuring of an effective plot. To achieve a well-paced story, the writer continually varies the speed of the narration, describing important events slowly in great detail and moving quickly over unimportant transitional material. Sometimes, however, beginners seem to feel that they should give equal weight to everything that happens, allowing as much space for telling how a character gets from one location to another as for the occasion that has brought him there in the first place. I recall, for instance, an exercise that a student wrote on the promising topic of a hot-air balloon meet, basing it on one that she had recently attended in Vermont with her husband and two children. Her description of what the child-protagonist sees and does after he arrives was interesting and colorful, but unfortunately she undermined the effect by prefacing it with a lengthy account of the unexceptional car trip that the family has taken to get there. But once the student adjusted the pace of the two sections, compressing the car trip into a single transitional sentence and stretching out the details of the balloon launching and flight, the piece became much more dramatic and lived up to the potential of the subject.

Throughout the narration, the writer must shed inhibition and be willing to expose the emotions of the characters to the public. Of all the qualities that caught my attention as a buying editor, it was the ability to write with genuine emotional impact that gave me most pause while reading a manuscript. A story that could make me laugh out loud or, more rarely, shed a tear in the course of a busy office day was one I considered carefully, no matter how flawed the plot construction or even character motivation. Often those more mechanical problems can be resolved with help in a revision, but only the writer can supply needed emotional power. I can remember reading a teenage novel in manuscript in which a parent died and the funeral service became an important scene. Though supposedly grief-stricken, the heroine never expressed her sorrow or lost her composure, because the author didn't want to distress her young readers. Unfortunately, she had protected them at the cost of reaching them. If no one in a story seems to care about what is happening, then the audience, whatever the age, is not going to care either. Writers who are concerned that their subject may be too strong for children should not attempt it, for weakening the impact will only weaken the drama.

Structure, immediacy, suspense, causality, pacing are all elements that go into the creation of a sound plot. Some take advance planning while others need to be kept in mind as the writing progresses. When new ideas occur, follow the inspiration of the moment and then go back to the beginning to see what adjustments will be needed to make the material fit. Perhaps they will be worth the effort and perhaps not, but the writer should be open to change as he or she becomes more familiar with the background of the story and the people in it. Setting, characters, and plot should each be part of the overall design while the narrative offers a continually shifting blend of description, dialogue, and action.

7

Choosing the
Right Genre

Picture books, short chapter stories, teenage novels. Biography, science and nature, social issues, how-to, language and art. Children's books not only deal with as wide a range of subjects in both fiction and nonfiction as adult books do, their format in terms of length and graphics shows more variety, as it is likely to be different for each category. Texts for picture books usually do not run longer than 1,500 words and are designed to share equal space with illustrations. On the other hand, an average length for older novels is 50,000 words, and these stories are rarely, if ever, illustrated. The so-called photo essay is the nonfictional counterpart of the picture book for the very young; it too has a short text and offers striking pictures. Nonfiction lengths increase with the age group, but photographs, diagrams, and sometimes original art continue to be important at every level. How does someone decide which genre is right for him or her when there are so many possibilities to choose from?

The starting point for most juvenile writers seems to be an interest in children of a particular age and then in the kind of book that is published for them. When I ask beginners what genre they want to write and why, most of the answers show the influence of their past experience in the home or on the job. A mother may find herself enjoying the bedtime stories that she reads to her children at night and feel that she has learned why some hold their attention more successfully than others. A fifth-grade teacher may have read aloud to her class for a number of years and developed an enthusiasm for the literature available to the age group. A young adult librarian has become expert in teenage reading tastes and wants to make use of his hard-won knowledge. How the experience was gained doesn't matter, but what *is* important for the aspiring writer is to have a specific sense of audience, which will then act as a guide in subject matter and style of presentation. Those who have only a vague idea of writing for children in general seem far more unsure of themselves and of their material.

Of course, this sense of audience sometimes comes from within, from the recollection of a few certain childhood years that still remain vivid to the writer for one reason or another. An author of books for teenagers once told me that she wrote for this age group because of her bitter memories of high school social life. A polio child, she was left with a limp that was barely noticeable to adults, but during high school it was apparently enough to exclude her from all dates and dances. Although the bitterness faded in time, the experience did provide her with total recall of those adolescent years that later earned her a wide and devoted audience. Often the most emotionally troubled times are the ones best remembered, as in the instance of a child who transfers to a different school when the family moves and finds herself unable to make new friends. If the aspiring writer can pick out a similar pivotal period in his or her own childhood, it may very well prove to be a productive vein to draw on.

Frequently, however, beginners do not take the next step of studying the formats of the books written for their selected age group to see if they offer scope for the kind of writing they do most easily. For example, the text of a picture book is a highly specialized form of fiction, more like poetry than storytelling in its tightness and rhythmic control. The writing must lend itself to illustration, which means that action will probably dominate description and dialogue, since backgrounds and conversations are difficult to make interesting in a picture. So those whose strength lies in description or subtle characterization may find that the picture book doesn't suit their talents, even though they have had considerable experience with this young audience, often designated as ranging from the age of four to eight.

There are other constraints imposed by the picture book format as well. Just as the number of words in the story needs to be limited so must the number of scenes, and a helpful model for many is the structure of a three-act play. If the writer presents the problem in the first act, builds it to a climax in the second, and resolves it in the third, he should be able to achieve the cohesiveness necessary to the form. Subject matter has its limitations too as the topic should be one that young children can identify with, such as a family relationship or a domestic animal. Fairy tales featuring unknowns like princesses and dragons or the frightening concept of the wicked stepmother are apt to appeal to an older taste. Lastly, because the books are often read *to* rather than *by* children, the writer must find special ways to allow them to participate in the story. One effective device, used in a number of favorite picture books, is the repetition of a key word or phrase, which the listener can chant along with the reader. For example, the rhythmic refrain of Omumbo-rombonga, the name of a sought-after fruit tree, is what makes the African folktale *Tortoise's Dream* by Joanna Troughton a never-fail hit in my local librarian's story hour. Thus, in all three elements of structure, theme, and style, picture book writing has singular characteristics that set it apart from other categories.

As children grow older, the books that they read become much more diverse in format. The next level is often referred to as the middle grade story, for roughly eight- to twelve-year-olds, and with exceptions at both ends it can range in length from 10,000 to 30,000 words. Most are illustrated, but far more sparingly than the picture book and almost always in black and white, since color printing becomes more expensive as the number of book pages increases. Now the writer divides the text into chapters, giving the reader stopping places and signaling pauses in the story. Some may be very short, intended for the beginner, while others may be a dozen pages or more, but all need to end with the promise of something interesting to come.

A book in which the author manages her chapter endings with great skill, making the reader want to turn the page immediately, is *The Midnight Fox* by Betsy Byars. The plot concerns a town boy's reluctant summer on a family farm, and how it unexpectedly turns into an enjoyable sojourn when he sights and becomes familiar with a wild rare black fox. All goes well for the first half of the story, but then the tenth chapter ends with a description of the notches Tom puts on his suitcase for each fox sighting and the explanation he will later give for them to his mother.

> After I got home, my mom said, "What on earth happened to your brand-new suitcase? There are notches all over it."
> And I said, "Let me see," as if I was surprised too, but if I had wanted to, I could have sat right down then and told her about every one of those notches, that this one was for when I saw the black fox carrying home a live mouse so her baby could start learning to hunt for himself, and that this one was for when I saw the fox walking down the stream, her black legs shining like silk, and this one was for when the fox passed me so closely that I could have put out my hand and touched her thick soft fur. The fifteenth notch I never put in the suitcase, for that was not a happy memory like the others but a painful one.

This bit of forecasting is subtle enough not to give away the plot in advance, yet it lets the reader know that something dramatic lies ahead and arouses his curiosity about what it might be. If he must put the book down at the end of this chapter, there is no danger of his not picking it up again.

With subject matter that is just as diverse as its format, the middle grade story can provide a springboard for all the various writing skills. *The Midnight Fox* combines setting (the farm and surrounding woods), characterization (the fearful boy who develops a love and appreciation of wildlife), and action (the activities of the fox) in almost equal measure, but that balance is rare. Most writers are stronger in one of these techniques than in the other two, and once they have acquired this self-knowledge, they should be able to choose the genre that features their special talent. For example, setting—the re-creation of another time or place—is of prime importance in historical and regional fiction as well as science fiction and fantasy. Character development is a key ingredient in school and family stories, romances, or any psychological study. Inventive and suspenseful plotting, in which the action is paced to create a number of dramatic high points, is needed in mysteries, adventure tales, sports stories. If beginners are unsure of what they do best, then they would be wise to take the time to read widely in the various categories and experi-ment with the possibilities.

Fiction for older readers, often listed as those age twelve and up, takes in as wide a range of subject matter but is a third again as long. Another distinguishing factor is that, in the words of one editor, it "jumps the great divide of pu-berty," changing the portrayal of relationships among the characters, particularly the sexes. A style that has become especially associated with this readership is one that features breezy repartee, demonstrating the author's knowledge of how the peer group being dramatized thinks and talks.

A lively example is the work of Walter Dean Myers, who uses this form to write about the social life of middle-class black adolescents. In *Won't Know Till I Get There*, the protag-onist, his two friends, Hi-Note and Patty, and his foster brother, Earl, are arrested by the transit police in a scene that is a comedy of errors. On the way home, the four teenagers discuss the incident:

> "They can't do nothing to us, really," Hi-Note said.
> "All we did was to put a name on the side of a train. That ain't no big deal."

"*You did what?*" Earl stopped and looked at Hi-Note, and Hi-Note took a step back.

"We put a name on a train," Hi-Note said.

"No, man." Earl fished a toothpick out of his pocket and put it in his mouth. "What you did was to Vandalize a Train. You a vandal! Not only that, but you told them you did it to a lot of trains, right?"

"Yeah."

"What I would do if I was you would be to get the rest of your boys to go around and clean off all the other Royal Visigoth signs you got up."

"What boys?" Patty asked.

"The rest of the gang," Earl said.

"What gang?"

"Them Visigoths, man," Earl said.

"I told you when I started writing it that that's what I *would* name a gang *if* I had one."

"So if you don't have a gang called the Visigoths, how come you go around putting the name on all those cars?"

"We don't," Hi-Note said. "We didn't know they were cops so we just made it up."

"You mean I'm in trouble because of what the gang you ain't got didn't do?"

I guess we all are, with a capital "T."

Because of the popularity of authors such as Myers and others like Ellen Conford, Norma Klein, and Paul Zindel, an accurate ear for adolescent speech is often associated with writing for this audience. In the book world, the writer gains group acceptance by learning the nuances of its language just as the teenager does in the real world.

In addition to all these levels of juvenile fiction, a wealth of nonfiction is published for children and read by them for pleasure. Biography has long been a staple of the literature, and today writers like Jean Fritz and Milton Meltzer are bringing new distinction to the genre with titles such as the former's *And Then What Happened, Paul Revere?* and the latter's *Columbus and the World Around Him*. They are showing that juvenile biographers can work to the highest standards of historical accuracy while at the same time making the writing lively and colorful enough to attract a wide audience of young readers. In the past, many children's biographers fictionalized their material, freely inventing dialogue for added immediacy, but this technique produced so many slipshod books that it has fallen into critical disfavor. My advice to beginners who are worried that the lack of conversation in a biography will bore children is to trust their subject. If they succeed in conveying what drew them to it in the first place, they will hold the reader's attention without having to resort to fictional embellishments that have no basis in fact.

Another pitfall for juvenile biographers is the tendency to emphasize the virtues of the subject and ignore the faults, that is, writing what is called "hagiography," the life of a saint. In their desire to present the young with role models, writers sometimes become reluctant to admit that influential historical figures have made mistakes and given in to weaknesses. But a person who has overcome grave problems to reach a goal is much more dramatic and believable than someone who accomplishes it without conflict. In her biography *Make Way for Sam Houston*, Jean Fritz does not flinch from the dark side of her hero, and yet his stature is not diminished by her "warts-and-all" treatment. Houston was troubled by alcoholism and bouts of depression that sidelined him from public activity during several periods in his life. That he recovered each time and eventually matured into the judicious leader of the Battle of San Jacinto, which established the Republic of Texas, is what makes his story interesting, not that he was a fearless outdoorsman and fighter. A biography glorified for the young gives them false information and is likely to be bland reading matter as well.

Admittedly, controversial views of revered public figures are editorially less welcome in broadly marketed biography series than in single titles, but critical standards throughout the genre are tightening. In a review that appeared in *School Library Journal* several years ago, the reviewer praised the series she was examining for avoiding "those banes of biographies for children: fictionalizing, premonition and hagiography," and writers who want to make a name for themselves as biographers would be wise to do the same. If research turns up material that they feel is unsuited for children, my advice is not to take the subject on rather than attempt a sanitized, incomplete portrait.

Length and structure of the biography will vary, of course, according to the age of the reader it is being published for. If it is intended for children in the early elementary grades, it may be only 5,000 words, and the author will have to be highly selective in the material that he or she includes. As an editor, I looked for treatments that focused on the crucial years in the subject's life and did not overemphasize his or her childhood as a crutch to enhance reader identification. I also preferred a straightforward chronological development that opened with the beginning of the story: usually when and where the person was born. Sometimes writers feel they should begin with a dramatic moment, no matter when it occurred, in order to catch the reader's attention immediately. The danger, however, is that the suspense of the narrative may be undermined by the revelation of what is to come and that readers may be confused by the more complicated time transitions.

Closely related to biography is the category of history, which has produced some influential books for the young. Because a textbook writer takes a neutral stance on controversial matters and gives both sides of the question, some seem to believe that the general writer should do the same. But the general book is one of several available, and its viewpoint can be balanced with others on the subject, so most agree now that this author has more latitude to express personal opinion as long as he does not present it as fact. Certainly overly cautious handling of material can result in very dull reading, and the most interesting books are likely to be those in which the author has a definite point of view, using it to interpret past events and to reach conclusions.

I learned how an informed and lively writer can transform

a dry history into exciting reading from working with the late historian and journalist Gerald W. Johnson. His trilogy *America Is Born*, *America Grows Up*, and *America Moves Forward*, which spanned the political past of the United States from Columbus to Eisenhower, aroused some concern when first published because of his outspoken judgments on people and events. "Harding was the worst President the country had had in many years"; "Woodrow Wilson knew that the guilt clause was untrue and that the reparations clause was foolish, yet he signed the [Versailles] treaty." But children found the books stimulating, and reviewers appreciated his ability to make the material sound "fresh and exciting again." In the end, the books were both a commercial and critical success (*America Is Born* and *America Moves Forward* were designated Newbery Honor Books), and Johnson proved his point that history for the young does not have to be passionless.

Today historical and social issues of every kind are addressed by children's books. Topics turning up in the review pages of *School Library Journal*, for instance, are likely to range from environmental pollution to teenage suicide, drug wars, child abuse, and social welfare. Not all will be of interest to every age group, of course, and writers should weigh carefully who their most likely audience will be in order to decide on an appropriate length and complexity of treatment. A guide that I found helpful when considering a manuscript was the school curriculum. At what grade level are students introduced to the subject and thus receptive to material on it? Social studies, to take one example, usually starts with the community and graduates to the less familiar arenas of state, country, and the world. A title on firefighting, therefore, would suit an early elementary child best while one about apartheid in South Africa would be better for a junior high schooler.

Books about distant places and peoples continue to be published widely for children, but standards of accuracy have tightened for them as for other forms of nonfiction. What editors and reviewers most prize is first-hand research, so writers who have lived in an interesting region or are able to visit one have an advantage in this genre. Travel writing can be a painstaking business as I know from the author Lila Perl, who described to me exactly how she went about gathering information for her titles on China, Mexico, Egypt, and others that I edited. After reading extensively on the country for several months, she then traveled through it for three or four weeks with an outline in hand of what she wanted to see. Each night she wrote up her day's observations, which sometimes took as long as four hours, and on her return home she indexed all the notebooks that she had accumulated. Only at that point was she ready to begin drafting the manuscript. No wonder that books by those who work solely from secondary sources suffer in comparison and have much less chance of success.

Perhaps the most heavily published nonfiction category in American juvenile literature is science and nature, which in recent years has broadened from zoology and biology to include a number of other subjects such as astronomy, geology, physiology, and anthropology. Of the many formats in this genre, an especially popular one developed for elementary age children is the single species book, consisting of a well-illustrated text of 5,000 words or so written about a specific kind of animal. Fathered by science writer Herbert S. Zim, the concept grew out of his observation as a science teacher that the most effective way to interest children in a topic is to start with concrete information and lead up to abstract conclusions gradually. Applying this approach to writing for the young, he chose limited, familiar subjects for his books, placing them in an overall context at the end. In contrast, adult nonfiction is more apt to open with a general introduction and then narrow to the specific concern. Beginning with *Goldfish* and other titles on common pet animals, Zim later explored less tangible sciences with books such as *The Sun* and *Your Heart and How It Works*, writing more than forty all together. Highly successful, the pattern became standard for middle grade readers and is still much used today.

A nature book format that also appeals to the young reading taste for the specific is the life-cycle story. In it, the author focuses on one particular animal, giving him a name (often based on the scientific species name) and following his activities from birth to reproduction. Though partially fictional in technique, the life cycle is still classified as nonfiction because the behavior that it portrays is factually accurate in every respect; the creature-protagonist neither does anything nor communicates in any way impossible for its kind. The writer Robert M. McClung, who worked for seven years as Curator of Mammals and Birds at the Bronx Zoo early in his career, has made a specialty of the form, often writing about an animal threatened by extinction. *Thor, Last of the Sperm Whales*, for example, is a picture of a typical sperm whale's life that incorporates facts about the historical cycles in the global population of the species. To gain the authority needed for this kind of writing either a professional background like McClung's or considerable direct contact with the subject is often essential.

Perhaps due to the influence of television, the visual presentation of a nonfiction book has become very important to editors and given rise to the format known as the photo essay. Designed for the youngest readers, the photo essay combines a short, simple text with dramatic pictures and is especially effective with nature subjects. In botanical titles like *Cotton*, *Catnip*, and *The Amazing Dandelion*, for example, science writer Millicent E. Selsam and close-up photographer Jerome Wexler showed children the wonders of plant life hidden to the casual eye. Similarly the author Joanna Cole collaborated with Wexler on animal books that featured a view of rarely recorded behavior like a miniature dachshund giving birth to a litter (*My Puppy Is Born*, recently revised with new photographs by Margaret Miller) and a pet Indian python eating a live chick *(A Snake's Body)*. Other gifted photographers who have made a name for themselves with the photo essay, or the photo concept book, include Tana Hoban, Bruce Mc-Millan, George Ancona, and Richard Hewitt. For writer-photographers or writer-photographer teams, this genre of nonfiction is one to study and explore.

Whatever the subject or format, the keys to successful nonfiction writing are organization, pacing, and clarity. The order in which material is presented can help to explain a topic, by demonstrating cause and effect, as much as the facts themselves, so an outline is well worth the extra time it takes to prepare. The opening especially should be considered carefully as the writer must both introduce readers to the topic logically and catch their attention quickly. Sometimes the two needs may compete with each other as happened when Herbert Zim was writing his book *Quartz*. Among the photographs collected to illustrate the study were some beautiful color shots of quartz gems such as amethysts. They would make an eye-catching beginning, but putting them there would mean an awkward flashback later to the true start of the story: the formation and classification of this most common mineral. In the end, Zim found a creative compromise, but it took much thought and rearrangement.

Although *pacing* is a term commonly connected with fiction, it also applies to nonfiction. Treatments that contain long stretches of dense, abstract material are laborious to read, but if the writer interrupts them with an anecdote or specific example now and then, they become much easier. In effect, the pace of the presentation varies as it moves back and forth between passages requiring close concentration and islands of relaxation that are less demanding.

Whether the text is dealing with difficult or easy material, however, it must always be as clear as possible. Some writers like to set a newly finished manuscript aside to cool off for a while and then reread it in order to judge clarity. Others look for a nonexpert reader, a stand-in for the child, to go over it as a double check. Even when questions seem foolish or misguided, if they point to areas of confusion, then the author should rework them until satisfied that the problem is eliminated. Puzzled readers are never wrong; they either understand or they don't.

In fact, I believe that above all other qualities clarity is the hallmark of juvenile writing in fiction as well as nonfiction. The author is trying to establish maximum communication with the audience, sharing ideas and enhancing identification. In his autobiography *A Grain of Wheat: A Writer Begins*, written for middle-graders, Clyde Robert Bulla tells of his growing up early in the century on a Missouri farm. Though this age in which children had both the hardship and the freedom of a two-mile walk to school is far distant now, readers will be able to experience the way of life through the book because the author re-creates its sights, sounds, and smells with such transparency. As in the *Little House on the Prairie* books by Laura Ingalls Wilder, the author hardly seems to exist; the reader responds to the page directly.

With this clarity of observation comes emotional impact. A classic example of how the two elements work together is E. B. White's story *Charlotte's Web*, in which the spider Charlotte becomes the friend and protector of the pig Wilbur. A master of unpretentious, precise language, White makes this improbable relationship so real that Charlotte's natural death comes as a great sorrow. In words that show White's gift for mixing naturalistic detail with philosophic understanding, she tries to prepare Wilbur and readers in advance:

> ". . . . After all, what's a life, anyway? We're born, we live a little while, we die. A spider's life can't help being something of a mess, with all this trapping and eating flies. By helping you, perhaps I was trying to lift up my life a trifle. Heaven knows anyone's life can stand a little of that."

That White is also the coauthor with William Strunk, Jr. of the much-used handbook *The Elements of Style* seems to me no accident. The most enduring children's book authors are accomplished stylists, able to use words so clearly that they forge an emotional bond with readers. That is the goal for aspiring writers.

8

Finding and Working
with a Publisher

How should I submit my manuscript to a publisher? Which publishers should I send it to? Should I find an agent to represent me instead? Is a multiple submission, to several publishers simultaneously, acceptable? These questions are some of the ones that turn up most frequently at writers' conferences, and although there is no single clear-cut answer to any of them, beginners are right to concern themselves with how the process of publishing works. Those writers who take the time to study publishers and develop some sense of the individual differences among them will have a better chance of success, because they will be able to target submissions to editorial offices more knowledgeably. But there are no short cuts, and the writer must be prepared to accumulate this information gradually on his or her own, reading trade magazines, consulting marketing surveys and listings, joining critique groups, and attending conferences.

Despite the importance of market advice, however, aspiring writers should not let it influence their choice of genre or subject unduly. That decision should be based primarily on personal experience and enthusiasm, the ability to bring something special to the book that will set it apart from others, such as access to new research on a timely topic. Chasing trends after they become widely apparent inevitably leads to imitative work that duplicates already published material. Successful authors are more likely to be those who have found a particular area of strength and stay with it rather than those who believe they can handle any topic equally well and write to satisfy a perceived need. Only when the manuscript is finished does the market survey become useful and help the writer match publishers with the project in hand.

Yet admittedly juvenile writers practice a specialty that is not always covered in general media and so must make an extra effort to keep in touch with what others are doing in it. Nonfiction writers, in particular, should be aware of what is available on their topic and how the various authors have treated it. I still remember receiving a query letter from a newcomer asking whether I would like to read his manuscript on drug abuse and stating that a huge market existed for it because there was nothing else on the subject for children to read. Since the previous year had seen an explosion of children's books on drugs, the writer clearly was given to making unsubstantiated claims, and I declined the invitation. Not that finding an untouched subject is necessary; in fact, it can be a disadvantage. As a school curriculum coordinator once told me, "We can't teach a unit with one book alone. We need at least several." But all the books should contribute something different—in viewpoint, coverage, or whatever—so they are complementary and do not simply duplicate each other.

In the genre of biography, editors also keep a number of other market factors in mind when considering the acquisition of a manuscript. Is the figure too obscure to be of general interest, or has he received so much attention that nothing more seems needed? Do the person's accomplishments relate to present-day issues, or do they concern problems that no longer matter to readers today? If the subject is still alive, will approval of the manuscript be necessary, and does the author have access to assure a reading? Sometimes a current social debate can bring new prominence to a previously overlooked figure, and the writer first to make the connection finds an unexpectedly saleable subject. For example, I published a biography of Paul Gauguin's grandmother, whose name was Flora Tristan, though I had never heard of her before, because the author had discovered in her flamboyant life a largely ignored source of feminist and socialist thought that made a relevant story for today.

Not only should beginners keep abreast of which companies are publishing what, they should learn something about how a book is put together in order to present their submissions properly. A common misconception is that a picture book must be complete, with all the illustrations in place, when it is sent to a publisher. Instead, the reverse is true, and unless the writer is the illustrator as well, editors far prefer to see a picture book text in manuscript form alone rather than accompanied by art prepared by an unknown on speculation. Book illustration has become a highly exacting profession, and since publishers rarely have the time to teach someone the desired reproduction technique on the job, it usually requires previous schooling. The chances of an unpublished writer being able to find someone with the necessary expertise willing to work without a contract are so marginal that editors advise against trying. They are trained to see the pictorial potential in a manuscript and maintain extensive files of samples from artists interested in assignments, so are well-equipped to select the illustrator for a story. Furthermore, a pairing made in the editorial office may give a newcomer the added benefit of an artist with an already established reputation that will enhance sales.

A frequently discussed question among writers is how much collaboration they can expect with the illustrator who is given their story to complete. Though the short answer is very little, which some find dismaying, in my experience the situation is apt to vary from book to book. At first, the editor is cautious because she doesn't know how professionally the author will be able to judge the art and how cooperatively he or she will work with the artist. Still, my practice was to put the two together quickly on nonfiction projects, because often the writer was the one best able to direct the illustrator to needed reference sources. I recall once, however, that an artist called me after a single conversation with the author to say that she was dropping the job. She had found his attitude so unpleasant that she was unwilling to work on his book any further, and though I tried hard I was unable to change her mind. Not surprisingly, in that instance, I did not risk letting that particular author work directly with an artist again. On the other hand, I can also remember a relatively new fiction writer showing such broad knowledge of current illustration that she soon came to play an important role in the selection of the artist for her work. The writer who learns how to contribute to the production process and speed it up is likely to become part of it while the one who causes complications and slows it down is not.

The standard presentation of manuscript submissions in all categories is to type two copies of the material double spaced on one side of the sheet (or print them out on a word processor), mailing the first and keeping the second. In addition, if the picture book writer has a specific plan for pacing the story, he or she may want to prepare a rough dummy that shows what text goes on each page. The space set aside for art can either be left blank or suggestions for content can be written in. The writer-illustrator also supplies sketches of the pictures for each page, but most publishers do not want to receive original finished art in the mail, because it cannot be replaced if lost. Photographs, however, are a different matter and, if available, will enhance the photo essay as well as longer nonfiction projects. Though not essential, a cover letter giving the author's past credits, if any, and reasons for selecting the publisher is useful too. It should be kept as brief as possible, since editors want to save their reading time for the manuscript itself, but some clues to the writer's personality, in the signature if nothing else, are of interest. All unsolicited submissions should include return postage in stamps on an envelope large enough to accommodate the submitted material, often referred to as the SASE (self-addressed stamped envelope).

These days, when publishers report great increases in the volume of unsolicited submissions, the so-called query letter inquiring about editorial interest in either a proposed or completed project has become a valuable timesaver. No more than one or at the most two pages long, it should briefly describe the manuscript, give the relevant credentials of the writer, and explain his or her reasons for undertaking the work. At writers' conferences, beginners sometimes ask what they should do if they have no credentials, as if a substitute were possible. Of course it is not, and the writer who tries to make a lot out of a little, such as "the children in my neighborhood loved my story," is worse off than one who doesn't raise the subject in the first place. Another pitfall is to discuss the market that exists for the book and to advise the editor on how the publisher will be able to reach it. Unless the writer has something very specific to offer, such as a free mailing list, he or she should leave marketing analysis and procedures to the professional staff. Only they will know how much money is available to spend on the book, and they will want to decide how best to use it.

But querying a publisher is not always preferable to submitting a completed manuscript. Although policy can vary from company to company, the consensus seems to be that query letters are most useful in the case of nonfiction as they enable the editor to spot subject duplication immediately. If the writer's topic is the greenhouse effect, for example, and the publisher already has a book on the phenomenon and does not want another, then the editor can head off a futile submission by return mail. On the other hand, most editors say that reading and responding to a query letter about a picture book takes almost as much time as reviewing the work itself, so they do not find an advance inquiry helpful for this category. In between these two extremes lies the uncertain territory of longer fiction, and here there is little agreement. Some editors say that they must read a story in its entirety to come to any opinion about it while others find looking at several opening chapters and an outline a helpful screen. Without any specific information to the contrary, my choice would be to send as much material as is available, since editors can always stop reading whenever they have reached a conclusion.

Inevitably as the volume of submissions increases so does the length of time that publishers take to consider them. To speed up the process, some writers now send their work to several publishers at the same time in what is called a "multiple submission." At first, the practice was frowned on by juvenile departments, but slowly it has been gaining reluctant acceptance as agents have developed the technique of auctioning their important authors to a selected group of publishers and selling the project to the high bidder. Of course, the situation of the unpublished writer is quite different, and some observers feel that given the amount of competition newcomers face, they should not provide an editorial reader with the slightest reason to pass them over. In any case, publishers are presently split down the middle on whether to accept multiple submissions or not, the only point of agreement being that writers making them should say so in the cover letter.

Another problem arising for writers from the slowing down of the submission process is when and how to retrieve a manuscript after an undue amount of time has gone by. Some assume that if a project is not returned promptly and is kept for many months, it is being given special consideration, and they do not want to jeopardize the chances of acceptance by making follow-up inquiries. Unfortunately, the reverse is more likely true, and the department's system of handling unsolicited material has probably bogged down for reasons that have nothing to do with the submission—loss of key staff, corporate reorganization, vacations, or whatever. To help those caught in this situation, the Society of Children's Book Writers, a national organization for writers and illustrators of children's literature, has developed a guideline for its members to follow. It suggests that writers allow a publisher to hold a manuscript for two months before writing to ask about its status. If there is still no response after three months, they should write again and officially withdraw the manuscript from consideration whether or not it has been returned. In the view of the Society, this policy strikes a more practical balance between the needs of writers and editors than the multiple submission.

Of course, writers who are represented by agents are spared these concerns, and the two questions I am asked most frequently are, "Do I need an agent?" and "How do I get one?" For juvenile authors, there is no single answer as many juvenile editorial departments, in contrast to adult editorial departments, continue to accept unagented material. Undoubtedly, if an interested and established agent is available, he or she can be very helpful, but many writers report that finding an agent is as difficult as finding a publisher. Many also report that agents are unable to spend as much time on placing the work of newcomers as are the writers themselves. So my advice is to begin submitting whenever the work is ready and to search for an agent at the same time if the process becomes too wearisome. Listings of agents are available in the annual reference *Literary Market Place*, from the Society of Children's Book Writers, and from the membership rosters of both the Society of Authors' Representatives and the Independent Literary Agents. Agents who specialize or have staff who specialize in juvenile publishing will usually note it in these references. Remember that an agent may be more useful to writers after they start to publish, when their business affairs become more complicated, than before, so take time to find the right one.

In any case, the quality of the manuscript being submitted is more crucial to a sale than whether or not it is represented by an agent. Beginners sometimes hesitate to judge their own work and instead think they should send it to an editor for an opinion on whether it is publishable or not. But commercial editors are not teachers, and their reading time is limited, so they respond personally to a writer only when the project seriously interests them. The rest of the submissions are returned with a generally worded form letter or card that does not give any specific reason for the rejection. Unfinished writers have little chance of gaining helpful criticism from this time-consuming process and will be better served by turning to other quarters for help in perfecting their craft. Local critique groups, university-sponsored workshops, writers' conferences, all can offer constructive feedback on work in progress and are well worth joining whenever they are available. Only when a manuscript is as good as the writer can possibly make it should he or she send it out to face the competition.

Not all publishers are the same, of course, and beginners should take time to study them—their output and the markets they sell to—in order to decide which companies might be most interested in what they have written. For short stories, articles, and poems, magazines offer a promising outlet and often are said to be more open to newcomers as their work can be combined with that of more established names in a single issue. The major division among trade book publishers (as distinct from textbook, which rarely use unsolicited material) is between mass market and, for want of a better term, up market. While the former produces inexpensive books for large-volume sales, the latter does the reverse and produces high-price books for modest-volume sales. Mass-market books are sold in supermarkets, drugstores, chain book and discount stores, and these publishers look for material of broad, proven appeal, often for the younger age ranges. Up-market books are bought by independent bookstores and school and public libraries, and the subjects can be more specialized since they do not need huge audiences to be successful. Selling to both markets are the paperback companies, some reprinting material previously published in hard cover exclusively, others offering original work in series and single titles as well.

Yet these distinctions have begun to blur as publishers aim to become "full-service companies," adding new markets to their base. Hardcover publishers are establishing their own paperback reprint lines instead of selling rights to outside softcover reprinters while paperback companies are launching hardcover lines in order to develop their own sources of material. Each of these editorial programs is separate, identified by a different imprint name, and the writer must now learn imprints as well as the companies that publish them to direct a submission appropriately. For example, a manuscript sent to a hardcover publisher's reprint paperback imprint that does not buy original work has little chance of being read as usually it is returned to the writer rather than passed along to another department.

In addition to being sure that the imprint buys original material and reads unsolicited submissions, the writer should try to develop a sense of the editorial taste that it represents. Some lists may specialize in picture books, others in sophisticated fiction for older readers, while still others emphasize nonfiction. Looking at new books in the collections of bookstores and public libraries is helpful, and writing for the current catalog of those publishers that seem especially interesting can be a useful follow-up. Market surveys, giving preferred submission procedures, subjects and genres, and age ranges, are available from professional magazines like *The Writer* and *Writer's Digest* as well as the Society of Children's Book Writers. Information on editorial programs, including how many and what kind of books are published, and personnel who review art portfolios can be obtained from the Children's Book Council. *Literary Market Place* is a standard source for names and addresses. Reading the trade magazine *Publishers Weekly* is a good way to keep abreast of issues, events, and gossip affecting the work of editors, art directors, sales managers. The more knowledgeable writers become about the business of publishing the more likely they are to succeed.

Sometimes beginners worry about what will happen to a manuscript when it leaves their hands. Will a publisher steal their material? Should they go to the trouble of securing a copyright on it before putting it in the mail? I remember one woman who brought her manuscript into the office but took it away when told an immediate reading wasn't possible, because she didn't trust it out of her sight. Startled, I realized that she had mixed up her priorities; she was more intent on guarding her work *from* readers than making it available *to* them. In fact, a manuscript is protected under copyright law, and an established company can be expected to handle literary work submitted to it in good faith, making the danger of theft slight. So my advice to writers is not to get ahead of themselves in the submission process but to concentrate on the first goal of finding an interested reader.

When a publisher does offer a contract for a manuscript, what should the author expect to find in it? First, of course, is the method and amount to be paid for each copy sold, which can differ from company to company and from one form of publication to another. For example, magazines usually pay a one-time flat fee, often based on a rate per word, while book publishers pay a royalty, or percentage, of either the list price (amount paid by the ultimate customer) or net price (amount received by the publisher after discount to the intermediary buyer, such as the bookstore or book wholesaler). A standard royalty is 10%, and in the case of picture books, to which writer and illustrator are considered to make equal contributions, it is generally split between the two. Authors of nonillustrated books receive the full percentage, and if they have had successful previous sales, the royalty may increase, or "escalate," when the sales reach a given number of copies. Authors of shorter, illustrated texts may be paid a lower starting royalty because of the additional production expense. The publisher accumulates these monies from individual sales, paying them to the author at set intervals, and the contract states the timing (often every six months) and dates of the payments.

In addition, the publisher frequently offers an advance on signing the contract, a specified amount to be deducted from the royalties earned by the sales to come. The size of the advance is apt to vary widely, depending on the author's past sales record, if any, and the anticipated earnings in the next year or so. If the book should not sell enough copies to "earn out" the advance, the author is usually not required to make up the balance, though adding the word *nonreturnable* to the advance clause is a simple way to remove any doubt on this score.

Writers may also encounter some companies that offer to publish a manuscript if the author pays for the cost of production. They are called "vanity presses," and their contractual arrangements are entirely different. Whether the practice is ethical or not is a matter of debate (at times litigation) and centers on the issue of whether the company has an editorial staff and is equipped to sell the book effectively once it is printed. If a writer enters into such an agreement prepared to take the major responsibility for editing, marketing, and sales, then it may serve his or her purpose. If he or she expects the company to perform in the same way as a traditional publisher, however, then the results may be extremely disappointing.

For those whose primary interest is to ensure that a project is preserved in print—perhaps as a family record—and do not want to take the time to find out whether it has commercial potential, there is now a far cheaper alternative. Desktop publishing, using the electronic technology of a word processor and a laser printer, has made the process of self-publishing much more practical than before. The public library, yellow pages, or a nearby writers' group are some of the places that may be able to provide information about local businesses offering such services.

Another important area covered by a publisher's contract concerns the ownership of the subsidiary rights to the book and how the income earned from the sale of such rights will be shared. Among the major subsidiary rights are magazine (first or second serial, depending on whether the material appears before or after book publication), foreign, reprint (paperback, book club), dramatization (movies, television), and permission fees for excerpts (textbooks, anthologies). Reprint rights are likely to involve the most money, and traditionally the publisher holds them, splitting the income from their sale equally with the author. Second-serial and permission rights may also stay with the publisher, but the company share in their sale is usually smaller, perhaps 25% or even 10%. Authors with agents are likely to retain first-serial, foreign, and dramatization rights; those without usually grant these rights to the publisher, who then acts as agent and receives a specified share, often 25%, for the work done in arranging a sale. If the book has an illustrator who is also receiving a royalty and whose art is part of the sale, then all these author shares will be divided between the two.

Most of a publisher's contract is preprinted, what is called the "boilerplate," and since it is standard for all, newcomers stand to gain little by questioning it. Those items that are considered negotiable are left blank and filled in after the individual agreement is reached. For example, the name of the copyright holder that will be placed in the book—usually the writer, but sometimes the publisher, who in either case will probably be the one to handle the registration—needs to be inserted to complete the copyright clause. In fact, the wording of the copyright notice does not affect subsidiary rights to the book or share of income, since these matters are all spelled out precisely elsewhere. But it can affect such long-range matters as responsibility for the book after it goes out of print and the contract is terminated or after the death of the author, and most advise writers to request a copyright in their name. Certainly the practice is wise for writers granting one-time magazine rights to a piece as they then can sell the same material elsewhere, to a book publisher perhaps, without having to ask the magazine for a formal transfer of copyright to their name.

Another matter of interest to newcomers concerns the arrangements for obtaining copies of their book. Generally the publisher provides a certain number—often ten, but sometimes the figure is negotiable—of complimentary copies on publication and then gives a discount off the list price on subsequent purchases. Frequently the discount is 40%, more or less a maximum for relatively small orders.

Although the writer should think of the manuscript as finished when submitting it for publication, the editor who responds with either an expression of interest or a concrete offer may very well be viewing it as a beginning. Most editorial readers expect unsolicited submissions to be flawed, or they would not still be available, so they do not look for perfection but watch for writing that reveals an original mind and creates an emotional impact. If they find a story that shows these qualities intermittently, then they may try to work out suggestions for solving the problems of the less successful sections and ask the writer to revise. Beginning writers at conferences have often asked me to interpret editorial letters for them, and distinguishing between those that are pleasant but noncommittal rejections and those that are real invitations to resubmit is not always easy. My rule of thumb is to judge by the specificity of the comments. If the editor does not want a resubmission as much as submission of future work not yet written, then the observations will probably be vague and hard to pin down. If the editor is seriously encouraging an immediate revision, then he or she will say so and the suggestions will be spelled out carefully enough to follow up or to decline.

In addition to revising the manuscript proper, other details may need to be settled before the process of book production begins. If the author has quoted material from other sources, will permission fees be necessary and who will pay them? In children's books, quotes from works of prose rarely exceed allowable limits, what is called "fair use," but even a single line from song lyrics and poetry can be expensive as it represents a large percentage of the whole. Usually clearing the permission is the author's responsibility, so the need for the material should be considered carefully. If the book is nonfiction, the editor may suggest a reading by an outside expert and ask the author for ideas on appropriate people, though the publisher will pay the fee. Does the book need an index and/or a bibliography, and if so, who prepares the material? A complex index for a long work usually requires a professional indexer, hired by the publisher, but a simple one for a short book may not need outside help, and either the author or the editorial staff may decide to take it on.

When a contract has been signed and a manuscript satisfactory to all is achieved, the book enters the production process. The first step is the copyediting—checking for accuracy of facts, punctuation, grammar, spelling—and if there is sufficient time, the writer is able to review the copyedited manuscript before it is sent to the compositor, or typesetter. Publishers would rather make adjustments at this stage than later on in type proof when each change adds to the cost of the typesetting. Next the text is marked up by a designer to indicate style, and the compositor sets the type from this master copy. It is then returned with the "galleys," as the sheets of proof are called, for reading by author and editors. To control the number of type corrections, authors are often given an allowance of 10% of the typesetting cost for changes without charge, although in some cases they may have to pay for all changes that are not typographical errors.

Coordinating the graphics of a book with the textual material is a special concern of juvenile publishing, and since the process takes technical training, it is largely carried out by the professional staff of the publisher. Perhaps, however, in works of nonfiction, and sometimes fiction as well, the author will be asked to check the artist's sketches for accuracy before finished illustrations are prepared. Even if the author doesn't see the interior illustrations in advance, he or she may have a chance to look at a proof of the jacket, with both type design and art in place, before it is printed, not for stylistic approval but as a final check against flagrant error. In the case of heavily illustrated books, the printer provides the editorial staff with blueprints ("blues") of each page so they can be sure that art and type fit comfortably together.

Printing and binding the book now takes place, and the immediate supervision of the job moves from the editorial department to the design and production departments. The production manager arranges for the delivery of a paper chosen for its color, weight, and cost to the printer, and a binding material that will coordinate with the jacket is selected. In the case of picture books, the art director with or without the illustrator often goes to wherever the printer is located to check the accuracy of the color reproduction as the pages come off press. Otherwise, contact is maintained by phone or through the printer's salesman, unless the publisher is one of the few with its own presses. Careful coordination is necessary both to ensure quality and to keep the work within the projected cost estimates.

While the book is still in production, the phase of marketing and sales begins. The marketing department sends out bound galleys to key bookstore and library reviewers, while the subsidiary rights manager alerts magazine, paperback, and book-club editors to the title. As soon as bound books are ready, advance copies are sent to the author, and several hundred review copies go out to magazine and newspaper reviewers, school and public library systems, perhaps to special-interest lists obtained by the publicist or supplied by the author. Now everyone waits to see how the buyers, retail and institutional, and then the children will receive the book. Although the manuscript has survived a winnowing process, in which it may be the only unsolicited submission published by a company out of as many as 12,000 received that year, it now will be evaluated at another competitive level. Current estimates are that almost 5,000 juvenile trade books are published annually, and neither review space nor purchase budgets are adequate to cover all. Certain titles will receive widespread attention, becoming hits of the season, while others will be passed over.

But fresh talent is the lifeblood of publishing, and editors know that they need new voices to invigorate their programs even as the field becomes more crowded. While an editor is held accountable for the sales that his or her books produce, the ability most admired within the profession is that of being able to spot the unrecognized writer. Furthermore, while the big well-known firms may have more submissions than they can handle, small new ones eager for material continue to emerge. For persistent writers, who come to their calling because of a real commitment to children and their reading, opportunities will always exist.

Appendix

Further Reading

Colby, Jean Poindexter. *Writing, Illustrating and Editing Children's Books*. New York: Hastings House, 1967.

Forster, E. M. *Aspects of the Novel*. New York: Harcourt, Brace and World, 1927, 1954.

Gates, Frieda. *How to Write, Illustrate, and Design Children's Books*. Monsey, NY: Lloyd-Simone Publishing Company, 1986.

Giblin, James. *Writing Books for Young People*. Boston: The Writer, Inc., 1990.

Litowinsky, Olga. *Writing Books for Children in the 1990's: The Inside Story from the Editor's Desk*. New York: Walker Publishing Company, 1991.

Roberts, Ellen E. *The Children's Picture Book: How to Write It, How to Sell It*. Cincinnati: Writer's Digest, 1987.

Seuling, Barbara. *How to Write a Children's Book and Get It Published*. New York: Scribner/Macmillan, 1986.

Shulevitz, Uri. *Writing with Pictures: How to Write and Illustrate Children's Books*. New York: Watson-Guptill Publications, 1985.

Woolley, Catherine. *Writing for Children*. New York: New American Library, 1989.

Yolen, Jane. *Guide to Writing for Children*. Boston: The Writer, Inc., 1982.

Zinsser, William, editor. *Worlds of Childhood: The Art and Craft of Writing for Children*. Boston: Houghton Mifflin Company, 1990.

Children's and Young Adult Magazines

Boys Life, 1320 Walnut Hill Lane, Irving, TX 75015

Chickadee Magazine (also *Owl Magazine*), 56 The Esplanade, Suite 306, Toronto M5E 1A7 Canada

Children's Better Health Institute (*Child Life, Children's Playmate, Humpty Dumpty, Jack and Jill, Turtle*), 1100 Waterways Boulevard, Box 567, Indianapolis, IN 46206

Cobblestone Magazine (also *Calliope* and *Faces*), 20 Grove Street, Peterborough, NH 03458

Cricket Magazine for Children (also *Ladybug*), 315 Fifth Street, Peru, IL 613544

Disney Adventures, Burbank Tower Building, 29th Floor, 500 South Buena Vista Street, Burbank, CA 91521

Highlights for Children, 803 Church Street, Honesdale, PA 18431

Hopscotch, PO Box 1292, Saratoga Springs, NY 12866

Kid City, 1 Lincoln Plaza, New York, NY 10023

Pockets, 1908 Grand Box 189, Nashville, TN 37202

Ranger Rick's Nature Magazine, National Wildlife Federation, 1412 16th Street, Washington, DC 20036

Scholastic Scope (list of 40 magazines published by Scholastic available on request), 730 Broadway, 8th Floor, New York, NY 10003

Seventeen Magazine, 850 Third Avenue, New York, NY 10022

U.S. Kids, 245 Long Hill Lane, Middletown, CT 06457

Professional Literature

ALA *Booklist* (also *Booklinks*), 50 East Huron Street, Chicago, IL 60611

Appraisal: Science Books for Young People, 605 Commonwealth Avenue, Boston, MA 02215

Bulletin of the Center for Children's Books, 1100 East 57th Street, Chicago, IL 60637

The Horn Book Magazine, 14 Beacon Street, Boston, MA 02108

International Reading Association, PO Box 8139, Newark, DE 19714, Attn: *Children's Choices*

Interracial Books for Children Bulletin, 1841 Broadway, New York, NY 10023

Kirkus Reviews, 200 Park Avenue South, New York, NY 10003

Literary Market Place, R.R. Bowker, 245 West 17th Street, New York, NY 10011

Publishers Weekly, 249 West 17th Street, New York, NY 10011
School Library Journal, 249 West 17th Street, New York, NY 10011
Science Books and Films, 1333 "H" Street NW, Washington, DC 20005
Society of Children's Book Writers *Bulletin*, PO Box 66296, Mar
    Vista Station, Los Angeles, CA 90066
The Writer, 120 Boylston Street, Boston, MA 02116
Writer's Digest, F&W Publications, 1507 Dana Avenue, Cincinnati,
    OH 45207

Professional Organizations

American Library Association, 50 East Huron Street, Chicago, IL
    60611
Association of Booksellers for Children, % Ms. Caron Chapman,
    Executive Director, 175 Ash Street, St. Paul, MN 55126
The Children's Book Council, 568 Broadway, New York, NY 10012
Independent Literary Agents Association, 432 Park Avenue South,
    Suite 1205, New York, NY 10016
International Reading Association, 800 Barksdale Road, PO Box
    8139, Newark, DE 19714
The National Council of Teachers of English, 1111 Kenyon Road,
    Urbana, IL 61801
Society of Authors' Representatives, 10 Astor Place, 3rd Floor, New
    York, NY 10003
Society of Children's Book Writers, Box 66296, Mar Vista Station,
    Los Angeles, CA 90066

Bibliography

Children's Books Cited

Avi. *Romeo and Juliet Together (and Alive!) at Last*. New York: Orchard Books, 1987.

Babbitt, Natalie. *Tuck Everlasting*. New York: Farrar, Straus, Giroux, 1975.

Banks, Lynne Reid. *The Indian in the Cupboard*. New York: Doubleday and Company, Inc., 1980.

Bauer, Marion Dane. *On My Honor*. New York: Clarion Books, 1986.

Beatty, Patricia. *Charley Skedaddle*. New York: William Morrow and Company, 1987.

Blume, Judy. *Tales of a Fourth Grade Nothing*. New York: E.P. Dutton, 1972.

Brown, Margaret Wise. *Goodnight Moon*. New York: Harper and Row, 1947.

Bulla, Clyde Robert. *A Grain of Wheat: A Writer Begins*. Boston: David R. Godine, 1985.

Burgess, Gelett. *Goops and How to Be Them, A Manual of Manners for Polite Infants*. Philadelphia: Frederick A. Stokes, 1900.

Byars, Betsy. *The Midnight Fox*. New York: The Viking Press, 1968.

——. *The Summer of the Swans*. New York: The Viking Press, 1970.

Calhoun, Mary. *Cross-Country Cat*. New York: William Morrow and Company, 1979.

Cassedy, Sylvia. *Lucie Babbidge's House*. New York: Thomas Y. Crowell, 1989.

Cavanna, Betty. *Almost Like Sisters*. New York: William Morrow and Company, 1963.

Cleary, Beverly. *Beezus and Ramona*. New York: William Morrow and Company, 1955.

113

————. *Henry Huggins*. New York: William Morrow and Company, 1950.

————. *The Mouse and the Motorcycle*. New York: William Morrow and Company, 1965.

————. *Ralph S. Mouse*. New York: William Morrow and Company, 1982.

————. *Ramona and Her Mother*. New York: William Morrow and Company, 1979.

————. *Ramona Quimby, Age 8*. New York: William Morrow and Company, 1981.

————. *Ramona the Pest*. New York: William Morrow and Company, 1968.

Cole, Joanna. *My Puppy Is Born*. New York: William Morrow and Company, 1973.

————. *A Snake's Body*. New York: William Morrow and Company, 1981.

Colman, Hila. *Bride at Eighteen*. New York: William Morrow and Company, 1966.

Conrad, Pam. *Prairie Songs*. New York: Harper and Row, 1985.

Cormier, Robert. *After the First Death*. New York: Pantheon Books, 1979.

Danziger, Paula. *The Cat Ate My Gymsuit*. New York: Delacorte Press, 1974.

Fox, Paula. *Lily and the Lost Boy*. New York: Orchard Books, 1987.

Freedman, Russell. *Lincoln: A Photobiography*. New York: Clarion Books, 1987.

Fritz, Jean. *And Then What Happened, Paul Revere?* New York: Coward, McCann and Geoghegan, 1973.

————. *Make Way for Sam Houston*. New York: G.P. Putnam's Sons, 1986.

Haywood, Carolyn. *"B" Is for Betsy*. New York: Harcourt, Brace and Company, 1939.

————. *Eddie's Happenings*. New York: William Morrow and Company, 1971.

————. *Here Comes the Bus!* New York: William Morrow and Company, 1963.

Holman, Felice. *Slake's Limbo*. New York: Charles Scribner's Sons, 1974.

Hoover, H. M. *This Time of Darkness*. New York: The Viking Press, 1980.

Hurwitz, Johanna. *Aldo Applesauce*. New York: William Morrow and Company, 1979.

————. *Busybody Nora*. New York: William Morrow and Company, 1976, 1990.

————. *Hot and Cold Summer*. New York: William Morrow and Company, 1982.

————. *Much Ado About Aldo*. New York: William Morrow and Company, 1978.

Johnson, Gerald W. *America Grows Up: A History for Peter*. New York: William Morrow and Company, 1960.

————. *America Is Born: A History for Peter*. New York: William Morrow and Company, 1959.

————. *America Moves Forward: A History for Peter*. New York: William Morrow and Company, 1960.

Klein, Norma. *Mom, the Wolf Man and Me*. New York: Pantheon Books, 1972.

Konigsburg, E. L. *From the Mixed-Up Files of Mrs. Basil E. Frankweiler*. New York: Atheneum, 1967.

Ladd, Elizabeth. *Enchanted Island*. New York: William Morrow and Company, 1953.

Latham, Jean Lee. *Carry on, Mr. Bowditch*. Boston: Houghton Mifflin Company, 1955.

Lauber, Patricia. *Volcano: The Eruption and Healing of Mount St. Helens*. New York: Bradbury Press, 1986.

Lisle, Janet Taylor. *Afternoon of the Elves*. New York: Orchard Books, 1989.

Lowry, Lois. *Anastasia Again!* Boston: Houghton Mifflin Company, 1981.

————. *Anastasia Krupnik*. Boston: Houghton Mifflin Company, 1979.

McClung, Robert M. *Thor, Last of the Sperm Whales*. 1971. Hamden, CT: Linnet Books, 1988.

MacLachlan, Patricia. *Sarah, Plain and Tall*. New York: Harper and Row, 1985.

Major, Beverly. *Porcupine Stew*. New York: William Morrow and Company, 1982.

Marino, Jan. *Eighty-Eight Steps to September*. Boston: Little, Brown and Company, 1989.

Meltzer, Milton. *Columbus and the World Around Him*. New York: Franklin Watts, 1990.

Myers, Walter Dean. *Won't Know Till I Get There*. New York: The Viking Press, 1982.

O'Brien, Robert C. *Mrs. Frisby and the Rats of NIMH*. New York: Atheneum, 1971.

O'Dell, Scott. *Island of the Blue Dolphins.* Boston: Houghton Mifflin Company, 1960.

Paterson, Katherine. *The Great Gilly Hopkins.* New York: Thomas Y. Crowell, 1978.

———. *Jacob Have I Loved.* New York: Thomas Y. Crowell, 1980.

Peck, Richard. *Ghosts I Have Been.* New York: The Viking Press, 1977.

Perl, Lila. *Egypt, Rebirth on the Nile.* New York: William Morrow and Company, 1977.

———. *Mexico, Crucible of the Americas.* New York: William Morrow and Company, 1978.

———. *Red Star and Green Dragon, Looking at New China.* New York: William Morrow and Company, 1983.

Potter, Marian. *Blatherskite.* New York: William Morrow and Company, 1980.

———. *A Chance Wild Apple.* New York: William Morrow and Company, 1982.

Reeder, Carolyn. *Shades of Gray.* New York: Macmillan Publishing Company, 1989.

Robertson, Keith. *Henry Reed's Baby-Sitting Service.* New York: The Viking Press, 1966.

———. *Henry Reed, Inc.* New York: The Viking Press, 1958.

———. *Henry Reed's Journey.* New York: The Viking Press, 1963.

Sachs, Marilyn. *The Bears' House.* New York: Doubleday and Company, Inc., 1971.

Schneider, Joyce Anne. *Flora Tristan: Feminist, Socialist, and Free Spirit.* New York: William Morrow and Company, 1980.

Selsam, Millicent E. *The Amazing Dandelion.* New York: William Morrow and Company, 1977.

———. *Catnip.* New York: William Morrow and Company, 1983.

———. *Cotton.* New York: William Morrow and Company, 1982.

Sleator, William. *The Boy Who Reversed Himself.* New York: E.P. Dutton, 1986.

Thayer, Jane. *Gus Was a Friendly Ghost.* New York: William Morrow and Company, 1962.

Thompson, Jean. *Brother of the Wolves.* New York: William Morrow and Company, 1978.

Troughton, Joanna. *Tortoise's Dream.* New York: Bedrick/Blackie, 1986.

Tunis, John R. *Go, Team, Go!* New York: William Morrow and Company, 1954.

———. *The Iron Duke.* New York: Harcourt, Brace and Company, 1938.

————. *The Kid from Tomkinsville*. San Diego: Harcourt Brace Jovanovich, 1940, 1987.

van Iterson, S. (Siny) R. *Pulga*. New York: William Morrow and Company, 1971.

White, E. B. *Charlotte's Web*. New York: Harper and Row, 1952.

————. *Trumpet of the Swan*. New York: Harper and Row, 1970.

Wilder, Laura Ingalls. *Little House in the Big Woods*. New York: Harper and Row, 1932, 1953.

————. *Little House on the Prairie*. New York: Harper and Row, 1935, 1953.

————. *On the Banks of Plum Creek*. New York: Harper and Row, 1937, 1953.

Yep, Laurence. *Dragonwings*. New York: Harper and Row, 1975.

Yolen, Jane. *The Girl Who Cried Flowers and Other Tales*. New York: Thomas Y. Crowell, 1974.

Zim, Herbert S. *Goldfish*. New York: William Morrow and Company, 1947.

————. *Quartz*. New York: William Morrow and Company, 1981.

————. *The Sun*. New York: William Morrow and Company, 1953, 1975.

————. *Your Heart and How It Works*. New York: William Morrow and Company, 1959.

Articles and References Cited

Bunting, Eve. "Getting Through Those Miserable Middles." Society of Children's Book Writers *Bulletin*, September/October 1984, pages 6–7.

Cleary, Beverly. Acceptance of Garden State Children's Book Award of New Jersey for *Ramona and Her Mother* in April 1982. Unpublished.

Garis, Leslie. "Simenon's Last Case." *New York Times Magazine*, April 22, 1984, page 20.

Hill, Margaret. "In and Out of Flashbacks." *The Writer*, May 1986, page 10.

Hutcheson, Barbara. Review of *Florence Nightingale* by Angela Bull and other titles. *School Library Journal*, April 1986, page 84.

Juon, Sarah. "You're the Judge." *The Writer*, November 1986, page 8.

Miller, Arthur. "School Prayer: A Political Dirigible." *The New York Times*, March 12, 1984, page 17.

Paterson, Katherine. Acceptance of Newbery Medal for *Jacob Have I Loved* in June 1981. *The Horn Book*, August 1981, pages 385–393.

Sanhuber, Holly. Review of *The Bloxworth Blue* by William Corlett. *School Library Journal*, November 1985, page 95.

Singer, Isaac Bashevis. "I See the Child as the Last Refuge." *The New York Times Book Review*, November 9, 1969, page 66.

White, E. B. and Strunk, William, Jr. *The Elements of Style*. New York: The Macmillan Company, 1965.

References Used for Historical Information

Cullinan, Bernice E. *Literature and the Child*. New York: Harcourt Brace Jovanovich, 1981.

Huck, Charlotte S. *Children's Literature in the Elementary School*. Third edition. New York: Holt, Rinehart and Winston, 1976.

Sutherland, Zena. *Children and Books*. Seventh edition. Glenview, IL: Scott, Foresman, 1986.

Index

119